D1420363

J. G. SIMMS

William Molyneux of Dublin

J. G. SIMMS

William Molyneux
of Dublin

1656   *1698*

Edited by P. H. KELLY

IRISH ACADEMIC PRESS

This book was printed in the Republic of Ireland by
The Leinster Leader Limited, Naas, Co. Kildare,
for Irish Academic Press Limited, Kill Lane,
Blackrock, County Dublin, telephone 850922.

© Estate of J. G. Simms 1982

ISBN 0 7165 00 96 5

CONTENTS

ILLUSTRATIONS

ABBREVIATIONS

B.L.	British Library
Cal. S.P. dom.	*Calendar of state papers, domestic series*
Cal. S.P. Ire.	*Calendar of the state papers relating to Ireland*
D.N.B.	*Dictionary of national biography*
D.U.	Dublin University
H.M.C.	Historical Manuscripts Commission
P.R.O.	Public Record Office of England
P.R.O.I.	Public Record Office of Ireland
Phil. Trans.	*Philosophical Transactions of the Royal Society*
R.I.A.	Royal Irish Academy
T.C.D.	Trinity College, Dublin

PREFACE

WHEN Gerald Simms died in April 1979, he had just completed the final typescript of this life of William Molyneux. Apart from the compilation of the bibliography and the checking of quotations and references, all that he wished to add were a few details, mostly relating to the circumstances of Molyneux's death, that were to be found in the sections of the Locke-Molyneux correspondence that had been omitted from the published version. For supplying this information thanks are due to Dr E. S. de Beer, editor of *The Correspondence of John Locke* currently being published by the Clarendon Press, as also to Professor T. W. Moody for the benefits of his editorial skills in a careful reading of the text which Gerald Simms had hoped to discuss with him.

Publication has been made possible by a grant from the Grace Lawless Lee Fund, Trinity College, Dublin. The index has been prepared by Dr Simms's daughter, Mrs Lisa Shields, who together with her husband, Hugh, has helped correct the proofs. Assistance in selecting illustrations and checking out details has been kindly provided by Miss M. Pollard and Mr William O'Sullivan of the Library of Trinity College, Dublin; Mrs Muriel MacCarthy of Marsh's library; the Photographic Services Department of Trinity College, Dublin; and Mr F. H. Aalen, Dr David Berman, Dr Toby Barnard, Professor H. M. Bracken, Dr Andrew Carpenter, Professor K. G. Davies, and Dr David Dickson. Mr Michael Adams has proved a remarkably forbearing and encouraging publisher.

P. H. KELLY   Trinity College, Dublin
                                                        March 1982

I

THE MOLYNEUX FAMILY

WILLIAM MOLYNEUX made his mark in many ways. To eighteenth-century readers in England, and farther afield, he was known as the friend of the philosopher John Locke, and as the writer of intelligent letters that made a substantial part of *Some familiar letters between Mr Locke and several of his friends.* By Henry Grattan and his fellow-patriots in Ireland Molyneux was revered as the author of *The case of Ireland's being bound by acts of parliament in England, stated,* the much-quoted textbook of colonial nationalism. Philosophers still discuss the Molyneux problem of the blind man who gains his sight and is confronted by the sphere and cube that he had previously learned to recognise by touch. In his lifetime he was an enthusiastic devotee of the new learning: a fellow of the Royal Society of London, an amateur astronomer who gained the regard of Flamsteed and Halley, a contributor to scientific journals in England and on the Continent, the author of the first substantial book in English on optics. In the Ireland of his time he was well known as an administrator and politician, as an indefatigable seeker after all kinds of knowledge, and as the driving force in the Dublin Philosophical Society, which he established as a sister institution of the Royal Society.

William belonged to the fourth generation of Molyneuxs in Ireland, and by his day the family had become part of the protestant establishment that dominated the social and political life of the country.[1] Marriage alliances had linked them to many of the prominent families that had settled in Ireland both before and after the sixteenth-century reformation. They thought of themselves as the English in Ireland, but they also thought of Ireland as their country. His family meant a great deal to William Molyneux. The position they had established in Dublin society gave him the self-confidence that allowed him to associate, and argue, with eminent men in other countries; the prosperity of the family enabled him to live the life of a virtuoso without having to worry about having to make a living.

Thomas, the first of these Molyneuxs to come to Ireland, had an unusual career. He was born in 1531 into the English community in

Calais. As his parents died while he was still a child he was brought up by another citizen of Calais, and appears to have prospered there until the French captured the town in 1558. He ransomed himself and was allowed to leave for Bruges, where he married the burgomaster's daughter, begat two sons, and seemed destined to become a Flemish burgher. But he and his family adhered to the reformation, and the Spanish inquisition made life hard for them. In 1568 they left for England, and in the latter part of the 1570s moved on to Ireland, where Archbishop Loftus of Dublin was ready to help protestant refugees from the Continent to settle and swell the numbers of the small protestant community. The archbishop's town of Swords in County Dublin was made into a borough in 1578 for the benefit of 'Thomas Molyneux, his wife, children and family and so many strangers as he should induce to inhabit'.[2] Thomas became controller of victuals in Dublin and appears to have been an efficient administrator. In 1590 he was rewarded with the office of chancellor of the exchequer of Ireland.[3] He evidently had the head for figures that characterised a number of his descendants. He also had the kidney trouble that was a family failing. A large stone from his kidney, mounted in silver with the inscription *A domino factum et mirabile fuit,* was at one time in the museum of Trinity College, Dublin, from which it has regrettably vanished. Thomas prospered in Dublin, taking lands on lease from the crown He lived at Thomas Court in the liberties to the west of the city' and also rented the archbishop's country mansion at Tallaght,' County Dublin. He is said to have lived expensively, dispensing bounteous hospitality to his large family circle. When he died in 1597 he left only a moderate fortune to his heirs.

His sons Samuel and Daniel were also prominent in Dublin life.[4] Both were members of the parliament that James I summoned in 1613. Samuel was surveyor general, in charge of buildings and works belonging to the crown. But he sadly mismanaged the office, leaving the work to deputies who cheated him. The result was that he fell heavily into debt and had to be rescued by his brother Daniel. Samuel, who was unmarried, died in 1625, leaving the line to be carried on by Daniel. The latter had become something of a scholar, proficient in Greek and the author of genealogical treatises, which he wrote while holding the office of Ulster king of arms in Dublin Castle, in the intervals of certifying pedigrees and dispensing heraldic emblems. The office had its hazards. An aggrieved gentleman, against whom Daniel had given an adverse opinion on a question of precedence, entered Daniel's garden with two servants and attacked and severely wounded him. He might have been killed if his cook

had not come on the scene with a red-hot spit and chased the
assailants. Daniel married Jane Ussher, a granddaughter of Archbishop Loftus. She was the daughter of Sir William Ussher, clerk
of the council and a member of one of the best-known 'old English'
families in Dublin, which included a famous archbishop, James
Ussher of Armagh. Daniel's sister Katherine married Robert
Newcomen, an administrator who became a baronet, and bore him
twenty-one children. The marriages of these children widened the
family circle so 'that there is hardly a considerable protestant family
in the kingdom to which they are not, one way or other, related. . . .
The tie of relation between the families of Usshers, Molyneuxs, and
Newcomens, became very remarkable, insomuch as they looked on
themselves but as one family.'[5] Daniel died in 1632.

His eldest son Thomas was a victim of the Irish rising of 1641,
which began in Ulster but soon involved the whole country in
prolonged warfare. While Thomas was in charge of Wicklow Castle
he was killed by the rebel forces in 1642, leaving one child, a
daughter. The second son William became a lawyer at Lincoln's Inn
and died unmarried in 1651. The third son Samuel then became
head of the family. His father had hoped that Samuel would become
a clergyman, and took care that he should learn Irish from his
nurse, the intention being that he should eventually be able to
preach to the people in their own language. However, Samuel did
not become a clergyman. He was trained as a lawyer and admitted
to the King's Inns, Dublin, on 7 February 1637.[6] His legal career
was interrupted by the war. He joined the army, which was com-
manded by the earl of Ormond, and distinguished himself as a
skilful artillery officer, making good use of a taste for mathematics.
He particularly impressed Ormond by his conduct at the battle of
Ross in 1643, where his performance was singled out for special
commendation. In the course of the battle Ormond 'caused the two
regiments posted at the mouth of the lane to open to the right and
left, and the two pieces of cannon to fire down the lane upon the
rebels' horse, which was done with so much care by Mr Molineux,
the chief gunner, that eighty men and horses were killed at the first
fire. The enemy did not care to stand a second, but set up a great
cry and hasted with all speed out of the lane into the open field
adjoining the ordnance playing continually on them, as fast as they
could charge and discharge.'[7]

The Irish conflict, which began as an insurrection of Ulster Gaels,
soon merged with the English civil war in what was known as the
war of the three kingdoms. Spasmodic fighting went on in Ireland
for twelve years before it was ended by the crushing weight of

Cromwell's army. It embittered relations between 'old English' and 'new English', catholics and protestants and, to a lesser degree, royalists and parliamentarians. Ormond, a devoted royalist, faced with the choice between Irish rebels and English rebels, preferred the latter and handed over Dublin to the parliamentarians. Most of the protestant citizens, Samuel Molyneux among them, stayed and after Cromwell's arrival continued in the service of the commonwealth regime. A list of the commonwealth train of artillery includes Captain Samuel Molyneux, 'master gunner of the field and firemaster'. There are also orders directing him to inspect military installations.[8] William Petty invited him to collaborate in the Down Survey, which mapped the lands seized from Irish catholics and allotted to Cromwellian soldiers and 'adventurers'. But Samuel, with some lack of perception, had insufficient faith in Petty's powers of organisation and declined the proposal. His brother Adam, who seems also to have had a talent for mathematics, took part in the survey.

During the war Samuel married Margaret Dowdall, daughter and co-heiress of a Dublin merchant who belonged to a protestant branch of an 'old English' family which was mainly catholic and in a previous generation had included an archbishop of Armagh who refused to accept the protestant liturgy of Edward VI. Her sister married Samuel's brother Adam, who also fought in the war in spite of having only one leg. He became a captain of horse and is said to have distinguished himself in many encounters, in the course of which he received numerous wounds: 'his face was so scarred, seamed, and the very bone of his forehead so broken with them that perhaps never any countenance wore more severe tokens of battle, and all thought it was wonderful how he survived them'.[9] After the war Adam was rewarded with an estate in County Longford and became a member for that county in the restoration parliament. Samuel and Margaret had a large family, but several of their children died young. William, born in 1656, was the eldest surviving son. His brother Thomas was born in 1661 and there were three daughters, Jane, Mary and Alice. Jane married Anthony Dopping, who became bishop of Meath and a leading light of the Church of Ireland. Mary married Dr John Madden, and Alice married her cousin, John Ussher. William and Thomas became closely attached, sharing the same scientific interests and outlook.

After the restoration Samuel Molyneux, together with a number of officers in Dublin, signed a loyal address to Charles II, dissociating themselves from the designs and practices of obdurate republicans and thanking the king for the restoration of the church and civil

government.[10] There was some restiveness on the part of rigid puritans against the return of the former order, but the 'old protestants' were glad to see the royal government return and they welcomed Ormond, now a duke, who was lord lieutenant for the greater part of the reign. Samuel engaged in some legal practice, but he refused the lucrative post of recorder of Dublin and was content to remain master gunner. This, in peace time, was a comparatively minor office, with duties of giving instruction in artillery and maintaining a register of guns. The going rate for the post was £190 per annum.[11] But it matched his interest in ballistics and his private income was adequate for his needs. He used to say that he kept the office for old acquaintance sake; he spent more than the salary on the experiments he made with the long gun and mortar. Apart from his interest in gunnery he is said to have been 'very curious in natural philosophy . . . [and] became an excellent philosopher as well as mathematician'.[12] He enjoyed the possession of a good library, to judge from the older books listed in the catalogue when the family library was sold after his grandson's death. His style of life was simple, directed to his own comfort rather than to the prevailing fashion; but he kept a good table and an open house for his numerous kinsfolk. He had the reputation of being uninterested in riches, leaving the management of his estate to his wife.

At the start of his married life Samuel was not particularly well off as his father had left debts, the result of standing surety for an irresponsible brother and of losing a law-suit with an aggrieved applicant to the Ulster office of arms. However, the opportunities offered to the protestant establishment in Ireland during the peaceful and expansionist years of Charles II's reign were such that he was able to increase the family fortune to a very substantial extent. The arrears of pay due to him for his army service since 1641 were met by the grant of over 1,000 Irish acres in County Limerick. To this he added the estate of Castle Dillon in County Armagh, which he bought in 1664 and which became the home of his descendants. Castle Dillon was named after the original English settler who got the land in James I's plantation. It was in one of the most anglicised parts of Ulster, with a hard-working protestant tenantry. The title was complicated and by the time sundry mortgages were cleared William reckoned that his father had paid £3,444—a very considerable investment.[13] Later on Samuel bought lands in County Kildare and elsewhere. These estates were investments, and it does not appear that he or his sons spent much time in them. In 1665 Samuel built a fine house just south of the Liffey outside the city wall, near Gormond, or Ormond, Gate, which became William

THE MOLYNEUX FAMILY

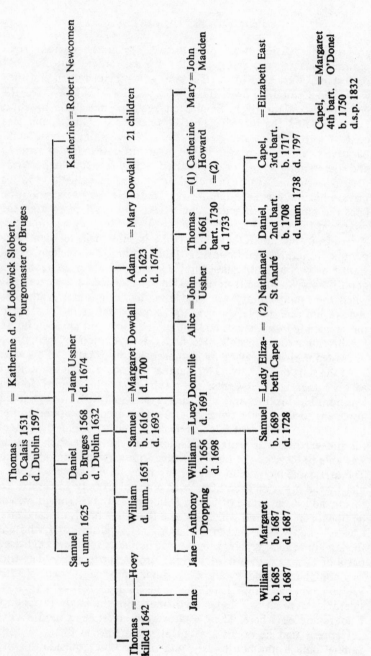

After the death of the 4th baronet the baronetcy passed to the descendants of the first baronet by his second wife. With the death in 1940 of the 10th baronet the baronetcy became extinct.

Molyneux's home for the rest of his life, with room for his books and scientific instruments.[14] The house is shown on Thomas Phillips's map, made in 1685.[15] There Samuel lived a patriarchal life, surrounded by members of his family and keeping 'a plentiful and a constant table'.[16] Samuel's wife Margaret was musical: a noted singer in her youth, and an expert player of lute, harpsichord and viol. She is said to have given an excellent training to her children, and to have been mainly responsible by her prudent care and management for the rise in her husband's fortune.

Dublin in the reign of Charles II was a good place to live in for families such as the Molyneuxs, comfortably off and with an assured place in the ascendancy network that controlled the administration and much of the economy. After years of war and tension it was a time of peace and prosperity. During the twenty-five years of the reign the city grew rapidly and spread far beyond its medieval boundaries. The population trebled, from about 20,000 to about 60,000, making it the second city in the British dominions.[17] It had the trappings of a capital: the viceregal court which, particularly under Ormond, was of considerable splendour, and the administrative and legal system appropriate to a separate kingdom. Its university was a miniature version of Oxford or Cambridge, though it consisted of only a single college. Among the administrators and academics were some men of culture with a taste for intellectual inquiry, and many of them were recruited by William Molyneux into the Dublin Philosophical Society. Although he sometimes complained of the shortcomings of Dublin, he was able to find in it some talented men who shared his mathematical and astronomical interests. He always referred to himself in his writings as William Molyneux of Dublin, and evidently took pride in the way the city had developed by the close of Charles II's reign: 'we are come to fine things here in Dublin, and you would wonder how our city increases sensibly in fair buildings, great trade, and splendour in all things,—in furniture, coaches, civility [and] housekeeping'.[18]

But the stability of Dublin protestant society depended on the support of the English government of Charles II who, whatever his personal tastes in religion, found it convenient to govern Ireland with the aid of a protestant ascendancy. The prospect would be very different with the accession of James II, a committed catholic, who was under strong pressure to entrust the administration to Irish catholics.

THE NEW LEARNING

WILLIAM MOLYNEUX was born in Dublin on 17 April 1656. He was a delicate child, afflicted with the kidney trouble that persisted on and off for the rest of his life. Of his schooling we know nothing more than the short account he gave his brother Thomas in an autobiographical letter: 'I was bred up at a grammar school, and can say no more concerning my behaviour there, but though I had over me one of the most severe school-masters in Dublin, I was never whipped at school for any idle or waggish trick'.[1] The school was probably that attached to St Patrick's Cathedral, which his brother later attended. On 10 April 1671, when he was almost fifteen, he entered Trinity College as a fellow commoner.[2] The Latin term *socius commensalis* indicates that he had the right of dining with the fellows on 'commons'. Other privileges granted to a fellow commoner, in return for paying higher fees, were the wearing of an impressively long and full gown, ornamented on the sleeves and edges with rows of tassels, and the right to obtain a bachelor's degree in three years instead of the usual four.[3] It was customary for a fellow commoner to present a piece of silver to the college, and it was duly recorded that William Molyneux had given a piece of thirty-two ounces. Hard times, during the unfriendly administration of Lord Tyrconnell, led the college to sell this along with the rest of the plate in 1686.[4]

Trinity College, Dublin, had been founded in 1592 with the object of providing education both to the English community and to a selection of the native Irish population. In the first half-century of its existence some catholics had attended, but by Charles II's reign its members were all expected to conform to the Church of Ireland. The endowment it had received from James I had been increased in the restoration land-settlement. The buildings, which are shown in Thomas Dineley's sketch of 1680 but all of which disappeared in the eighteenth century, were being extended during Molyneux's undergraduate days as the result of the benevolence of a judge, Sir Jerome Alexander. The number of students was about three hundred.[5] Two of his fellow students, St George Ashe and

Robert Molesworth, remained his friends in later life, and Ashe was closely associated with him in scientific work and the affairs of the Dublin Philosophical Society.

The curriculum was traditional, with disputations and Aristotelian texts the staple diet. The courses had been prescribed by Archbishop Laud forty years previously and had been re-established at the restoration in place of the more radical programme introduced by the commonwealth. Molyneux was repelled by the formal teaching provided in the degree course. In the words of one of his biographers he had 'conceived a great dislike to the scholastic learning then taught in that place and, young as he was, he fell entirely into Lord Bacon's methods and those prescribed by the Royal Society'.[6] He himself expressed his feelings in an account he later gave to his brother: 'I always had a strong bent and inclination to the philosophical and mathematical studies, even when I was in the university, wherein I could never approve of that verbose philosophy there professed and taught, but still procured the books of the Royal Society: the *Philosophical Transactions,* Descartes's writings, Dr Bacon's works, Gassendus, Digby etc. In these sorts of authors I chiefly delighted, even in my first academic studies.'[7] He did not say what influences led to his enthusiasm for the new learning. He did not give the credit to William Palliser, his tutor, a learned man with a fine library, who became one of the early members of the Dublin Philosophical Society but who appears to have been more interested in theology than in scientific matters. Surprisingly, he says nothing of the recently established lectureship in mathematics, the holder of which was Myles Symner, a devotee of the new learning, who had been chief engineer during the interregnum and had been a colleague of Samuel Molyneux in the commonwealth artillery train.[8] The terms of the lectureship included the obligation to give private teaching in mathematics to those students who desired it. It was probably from his father and his father's library that Molyneux got his inspiration. The bond between father and son was clearly very close and they shared many interests in common.

Molyneux was admitted bachelor of arts on 27 February 1674. He spent the following year at home and was then sent to London to study law. The college gave him a handsome testimonial to take with him, testifying to his talents and industry in pursuit of his studies. He was entered at the Middle Temple on 23 June 1675. He pursued his legal studies without great enthusiasm, being diverted by other interests and confident of his prospects of inheriting a substantial estate: he had 'an head bent on other studies more polite but less fruitful'.[9] However, he stayed the course and was able to bring home commonplace books filled with extracts from his reading of law.

He returned to Ireland in June 1678 and was at once involved in the arrangements for his marriage to Lucy, the youngest daughter of Sir William Domville, the attorney general for Ireland. Sir William was a successful lawyer who had bought a fine estate at Laughlinstown, about nine miles south-east of Dublin; he also had a house in Bride Street, which is shown in Thomas Phillips's map of Dublin.[10] At the time of Charles II's restoration he had written an important disquisition, in which he challenged the claim of the English parliament to legislate for Ireland. His son-in-law was to make good use of this disquisition when he came to write *The case of Ireland's being bound*. The marriage took place on 19 September 1678 in Laughlinstown House. It was celebrated by the bridegroom's brother-in-law, Anthony Dopping, who was at this time vicar of St Andrew's church in Dublin and entered the marriage in the register of that church. Molyneux makes it plain that he himself took the initiative in proposing the match, but it was clearly accepable to both families. He was delighted with his bride: 'I can say, she was looked upon as one of the finest faces in Ireland, neither was her mind in any wise disagreeable to her outward form . . . I thought myself the happiest man alive in my marriage to her'.[11]

But misfortune soon struck the young couple. A little over two months after the marriage—on Sunday, 24 November—as Lucy came out of morning service at Christ Church and was stepping into the coach she was attacked by a sudden convulsive fit. This was followed by 'the most dismal and tedious sickness'.[12] Within a month she complained of failing eyesight and by January 1679 her sight had almost completely gone; she could distinguish day from night, but nothing more. The loss of sight was accompanied by severe headaches and dizziness, and she was dogged by ill-health for most of the remainder of her life. She bore her illness, and the remedies prescribed by her doctors, with remarkable patience. Molyneux was filled with admiration for her general cheerfulness, and showed great understanding of her occasional fits of unhappiness. She was sent from one Dublin doctor to another and subjected to blisterings, cuppings, and other unpleasant forms of treatment, without result. Eventually Molyneux decided to take her to England, and they reached London on 11 June 1679. There Lucy was taken to a lady who was famous for her skill in treating diseases of the eyes, but who at once decided that Lucy's case was beyond her capabilities. The Molyneuxs had already been told of a Dr Turberville of Salisbury, who was a celebrated oculist, and Lucy was next taken to him. He gave her a disagreeable course of treatment which went on for over two months, with no success. The disheartened couple decided to go back to Ireland.

They spent part of the winter in Domville's house in Bride Street, Dublin, where Molyneux passed the time by translating Descartes's *Meditations*. This was published in London in the following April, together with Hobbes's objections, Descartes's replies to them, and a short account of Descartes's life. Molyneux was evidently particularly attracted by what he saw as the mathematical form of Descartes's thought. In the preface he referred to 'the physico-mathematical argument' of the meditations. The book was published by Benjamin Tooke at the Ship in St Paul's Churchyard. Tooke's connection with Dublin was no doubt the reason for his selection. His nephews, John and Andrew Crooke, were Dublin printers, and Tooke, as their trustee, had been included in the patent appointing them printer-general of Ireland.[13] A number of Dublin-printed books bore his name. Molyneux continued to make use of Tooke, not only as publisher, but as bookseller and general agent. His translation of Descartes's *Meditations* was an understandable recourse to the consolations of philosophy. The depression that he felt at this period may account for another piece of writing: a summary of John Donne's *Biathanatos, a declaration of the paradox or thesis that self-homicide is not so naturally sin, that it may never be otherwise*.[14] Molyneux also translated part of Galileo's *Discorsi e demonstrazioni mathematichè intorno à due nuove scienze* from the Italian. He did not publish this work, which was dedicated to his 'honoured and affectionate father'. He modestly disclaimed skill in Italian: 'I must needs intimate that I had not looked into an Italian grammar or other Italian author over three days before I undertook this work. This I am the more willing to prefix before the following sheets lest hereafter they may be viewed by some that may censure me for the badness of the translation. But these I will inform beforehand that I did this only for your private use.' He justified himself by claiming that his knowledge of Galileo's doctrine enabled him to perform the task better 'than one more skilled in the Italian and wholly ignorant in the doctrine'. A further reason for undertaking the translation was that all copies of Thomas Salusbury's translation had been destroyed in the Great Fire of London, so that none could be procured. In fact his translation is a creditable achievement.[15]

Lucy had not completely lost her faith in Dr Turberville and persuaded her husband to take her back to England in the spring of 1680. This time the treatment was given in London and continued till July without result. Dr Sydenham and other leading physicians were also consulted and pronounced the case hopeless. There was nothing for it but to return to Dublin and abandon the search for a cure. Molyneux came to what was almost certainly the correct conclusion, that Lucy's loss of sight was not caused by any defect of the eyes but was the result of a brain disease. He noted that her eyes remained bright and showed no signs of impaired vision. He later recollected that she showed extraordinary patience, which eased the strain felt by both families, and that she diverted herself with music and with handwork, in which she developed remarkable dexterity.

He himself found consolation in the study of mathematics, which he now took up in earnest. He recorded that he learned the rudiments of the subject from George Tollet, who was for many years well known as a teacher of mathematics in Dublin and who became a prominent member of the Dublin Philosophical Society. It was natural that he should have become particularly interested in optics. Apart from Lucy there was a blind girl in the Molyneux household, the daughter of Samuel's brother Thomas who had been killed in the turmoil of the 1640s; she found the kindness and care of a father in her uncle Captain Samuel Molyneux, in whose house she was brought up and provided for as one of his own daughters.[16] Optics was a subject that was then engaging the attention of a number of leading scientists—Isaac Newton, Christiaan Huygens, and others. With the study of optics went an interest in telescopes, micrometers, and other instruments, and in astronomical observations. For an enthusiastic amateur it was an exciting period of experiment and speculation in many fields of knowledge. Scientists in many countries of Europe were actively engaged in trying to solve similar problems in astronomy and physics. Their progress was recorded in a number of learned journals, and there was much rivalry and reciprocal criticism. In London Flamsteed, Hooke and Halley kept a jealous eye on one another's astronomical discoveries. In Cambridge Newton was at work on discoveries that would later form the basis of his *Principia*; he had also written, but not yet published, a considerable part of a treatise on optics. In Holland Huygens was producing important work on optics and astronomy. Leibniz in Germany was a pioneer of mathematics. Far away in Danzig Hevelius was studying the heavens without benefit of the instruments used by his fellow-astronomers in western Europe. The *Philosophical Transactions* of the Royal Society and the *Journal des sçavans* in Paris were the chief means of communicating the advances of science. Soon to be added to the list were the *Acta Eruditorum* of

Leipzig (1682), Bayle's *Nouvelles de la république des lettres* (1684), and Le Clerc's *Bibliothèque universelle et historique* (1686), both published in Amsterdam. Isolated in Dublin, Molyneux was an avid reader of journals and books, and corresponded with other workers in his field.

His first important achievement in astronomy was to record the progress of the lunar eclipse seen in Dublin on 1 August 1681. He sent his results to a friend in London, Charles Bernard. The latter was friendly with John Flamsteed, the Astronomer Royal, whom Molyneux had already visited at Greenwich Observatory. Bernard took Molyneux's observations down to Greenwich and showed them to Flamsteed. At the same time he asked Flamsteed to test a couple of lenses which Molyneux was buying. Flamsteed checked Molyneux's observations of the eclipse with his own, and found that six of the seven agreed closely, but that the seventh did not tally. He also took the trouble to examine Molyneux's lenses, which stood the test. He wrote a friendly letter to Molyneux, commending his work as 'better than I have commonly met with in the information of others', and telling him that he had given Bernard his own observations for despatch to Dublin. He hoped that Molyneux would be encouraged to continue with his observations, and he promised to help him in any way he could. Molyneux in his reply expressed his gratitude for Flamsteed's generosity and promised to take advantage of 'the help and advice of one of the most celebrated astronomers of Europe'.[17]

This was the beginning of a correspondence that went on at frequent intervals over the next ten years, in which problems of optics, astronomy, ballistics, and tides were fully discussed. Neither writer hesitated to offer criticism or ask for further explanation. Flamsteed was quite uninhibited in writing about other astronomers, and in all the letters that have survived expressed warm appreciation of Molyneux, which was no less warmly reciprocated. The length and cordiality of their friendship was remarkable as Flamsteed, whose health was poor and whose temper was prickly, had the reputation of being very difficult to get on with and sooner or later fell out with all his fellow-astronomers. How he eventually quarrelled with Molyneux will be considered in due course. Molyneux learned a great deal from Flamsteed, particularly in the selection and practical handling of instruments and in the solution of problems in optics. Flamsteed was glad to get Molyneux's observations of eclipses, satellites, and other celestial phenomena, and also to get information on the Dublin tides for incorporation in the tide-tables that he compiled.

Molyneux felt greatly handicapped by the lack of reliable instruments for astronomical work and had a poor opinion of Dublin artificers. He explained to Flamsteed that 'living here in a kingdom barren of all things, but especially of ingenious artificers, I am wholly destitute of instruments that I can rely on, but . . . I know, if at any time I send to London for some you will not deny me your assistance in choosing them'.[18] Flamsteed was most willing to help. He had a shrewd idea of the limitations of Dublin, as he had spent a fortnight there in 1665 being stroked for his ailments by the celebrated healer, Valentine Greatrakes. He understood that Molyneux was able to afford high-class instruments and proposed to get him a quadrant of two foot radius with telescopic sights at a cost of £12. Flamsteed tested the instrument, found it 'about five minutes faulty', and told the maker to correct it before supplying it to Molyneux. Unfortunately, he did not do so satisfactorily, and Molyneux was unable to use the instrument to observe the comet that became visible in Dublin on 19 August 1682. That was 'Halley's comet', and it would have been interesting to get Molyneux's observations of it. The correspondence also contains requests by Molyneux for Flamsteed's help in testing a telescope and a microscope ordered from Yarwell, a London craftsman. Molyneux sent Flamsteed a number of his observations on eclipses. Flamsteed compared them with his own observations and criticised any shortcomings in Molyneux's work, which was sometimes amateurish. For instance, on one occasion he admitted that an error in recording the beginning of an eclipse was caused by his being 'disturbed by company'.[19]

Flamsteed's letters to Molyneux are very friendly, and it was not long before he was writing to him with great frankness. In his letter of 11 April 1682 he gave Molyneux his views on Hooke, who was then secretary of the Royal Society. He criticised Hooke's failure to keep up the series of *Philosophical Transactions* that his predecessor, Henry Oldenburg, had produced: Hooke's *Philosophical Collections* fell far short of them. He had a poor opinion of the inventive powers for which Hooke was celebrated: 'I look on them as only boasts or a piece of contrivance to magnify himself . . . I write freely to you as to an intimate friend; you will therefore make use of it only to prevent your own errors or your acquaintances in their opinion and expectations of his prodigious promises.' Molyneux expressed his pleasure at being taken into Flamsteed's confidence and assured him that he would not betray it. He announced his complete agreement with Flamsteed's opinion of Hooke: 'truly I never harboured any great thoughts of that gentleman or his writings, wherein I could instance many great follies, besides that it is absolutely intolerable in any man to promise so much and perform so little'.[20]

Molyneux later became involved in the controversy between Hooke and Hevelius, the Danzig astronomer. Hevelius made his observations with open sights and claimed that his method was superior to the use of telescopic lenses. This claim was asserted in the first part of Hevelius's *Machina coelestis*, published in 1673. In the following year Hooke disputed the claim in his *Animadversions on the first part of the Machina coelestis*. In 1679 Halley went to Danzig to test the rival theories. He and Hevelius made a series of joint observations, using telescopic and open sights respectively. There were in fact discrepancies, but Halley was so ill-advised as to give Hevelius a written testimonial saying that their observations agreed to an almost unbelievable degree, differing only by a negligible fraction of a minute. He testified to the remarkable accuracy of Hevelius's instruments, challenging those who tried to cast doubt on them. Hevelius then proceeded to write a work, *Annus climactericus* (1685), in which he repeated his claim that open sights were quite as good as the telescopic sights used by other astronomers, and included Halley's testimonial and the results of their joint observations. He sent several copies to the Royal Society, which decided to give a copy each to the Dublin and Oxford Societies. Dr John Wallis, Savilian professor of geometry at Oxford, in a review of the book came down in favour of Hevelius's open sights, which annoyed the champions of the telescope.[21]

Molyneux presented the book to the Dublin Philosophical Society on behalf of the Royal Society on 9 November 1685, and made a number of comments on it. He was already familiar with the controversy and had read a discourse to the Dublin Society early in 1684, in which he had taken Hooke to task for the ill-natured manner in which he had criticised Hevelius.[22] At the presentation of Hevelius's book he seems to have spoken extempore, but at the following meeting, on 16 November, he 'read a large discourse containing his thoughts of Hevelius's *Annus climactericus* and the difference between Mr Halley's and Hevelius's observations'.[23] The substance of this discourse was given in a very long letter from Molyneux to Francis Aston, one of the secretaries of the Royal Society. It contains a detailed comparison of the observations that Halley and Hevelius made together and shows that there were very significant differences between them, in one case of eight minutes. He pointed out that Halley's testimonial to the accuracy of Hevelius's observations could only cast doubt on his own telescopic observations. Molyneux paid tribute to Hevelius's prodigious labours, but made clear his own position that telescopic sights were much more accurate than open sights. He apprehended that Hevelius's book would lead to a slighting of telescopic sights, and called on Halley to vindicate his own observations.[24]

Hevelius had written that Halley's instrument was a sextant, and Molyneux had concluded that it was the large instrument with which Halley had made observations at St Helena, and that he had made use of those observations for comparison with those taken by Hevelius. It turned out that Halley had taken a quadrant—a less sophisticated instrument—to Danzig, so that the St Helena observations were not on the same basis. Apart from this, Molyneux had written a penetrating review, bringing out the issues clearly and fairly. His letter was read to the Royal Society and a copy was given to Halley. Hooke's reaction was to complain that his *Animadversions* had been called a pamphlet. Molyneux asked Halley to assure Hooke that no offence had been intended; he had thought 'pamphlet' an appropriate term for a small stitched book. In writing to Flamsteed Molyneux said that if Hooke would not accept this explanation Molyneux could only say that it was 'a pamphlet in the worst sense, and that too a vain, bragging, scurrilous pamphlet'.[25]

Aston sent a copy of Molyneux's letter to the Oxford Society, but asked that it should not be printed, as so much ill feeling had been stirred up by Wallis's review of Hevelius's book. Molyneux's letter was read to the Oxford Society and its secretary proposed that Molyneux should translate it into Latin for Hevelius's benefit. This was done and the Latin version was sent to Danzig, with a postscript pointing out that Halley had used a quadrant, not a sextant. Molyneux was nettled at having been misled by Hevelius and told Halley that if he had not thought a sextant had been used he would hardly have put pen to paper. He thought Hevelius's account 'most disingenuously done'. He also thought that Hevelius had a very imperfect understanding of telescopic instruments.[26]

Halley was reluctant to defend the reputation of himself and the telescopic sights. He wrote to Molyneux: 'As to Mr Hevelius we hear as yet no further from him, and I am very unwilling to let my indignation loose upon him, but will, unless I see some public notice taken elsewhere, let it sleep until after his death, if I chance to outlive him, for I would not hasten his departure by exposing him and his observations as I could do and truly as I think he deserves I should'. Halley's indignation was caused by several references to himself in Hevelius's book: besides the mention of the sextant Hevelius said Halley had been sent to St Helena by the

Royal Society, whereas he had gone on his own initiative and at his own expense. Hevelius had also said that Halley had been sent to Danzig specifically to examine Hevelius's instruments, whereas Halley declared that the object of his visit had been to pay respects to a famous savant. Molyneux thought that Halley should speak out while Hevelius was alive and in a position to defend himself. He frankly told Halley that he would always be saddled with the testimonial he had given Hevelius: the alternative was that Halley had 'grossly flattered him and imposed on the world'.[27] Hevelius died in the following year and the controversy died with him. The episode is an example of astronomical in-fighting. It shows Molyneux in a favourable light, treating the case on its merits, expounding his views logically and clearly, not hesitating to tell Halley what he thought of him. Halley took the criticism in good part and they remained firm friends.

On 3 February 1686 Hooke gave the Royal Society a demonstration of two inventions: an improved barometer, and a level designed to establish a true horizontal line. Halley sent Molyneux a detailed description of the barometer which, by the use of spirits of wine and oil of turpentine as balancers, showed variations in the mercury more clearly than in earlier models. Molyneux replied: 'Mr Hooke's contrivance for the baroscope is admirably curious'. But he thought it would be difficult to manufacture. He told Halley that he had always had a great esteem for Hooke's mechanical inventions, 'of which I look upon him to be as great a master as any in the world'.[28] This is very different from the highly unfavourable opinion of Hooke that Molyneux had previously expressed to Flamsteed. The Dublin Society had also received a description of Hooke's level and asked Molyneux to examine it. He got a sample 'very nicely and accurately made', and explained its points at a meeting of the society. Although he thought the pendulum too inclined to oscillate 'he concluded all with great commendation of the inventor and invention, which received the applause of the whole meeting'.[29]

Galileo and his successors ensured that the problem of tides was one of the preoccupations of seventeenth-century philosophers, and it was of great interest to members of the Royal Society. Flamsteed, as Astronomer Royal, compiled annual tide-tables, published in the *Philosophical Transactions,* giving the time of high water at London Bridge for every day of the year. He appended to these the differences to be added or subtracted for other ports, including Dublin. In January 1683 he sent his tables to Molyneux and asked him whether there was a constant difference between Dublin and London and what were the differences of time for Dublin Bay and the Custom

House on the Liffey. He also asked for the times of high water at the spring and neap tides. If Molyneux could easily obtain the information, Flamsteed would like the times for Cork and other Irish ports.

Molyneux replied that he had made inquiries from an experienced seaman, but with disappointing results. He added: 'it is my misfortune that I live too remote from our river to make any observations myself'. This was a surprising remark, considering that he lived within a few yards of the tidal waters of the Liffey, though the actual port was further away. He thought that four hours should be subtracted from the London time to give high water at Dublin, whereas Flamsteed had subtracted only three.[30] Flamsteed did not accept this. The modern tables show two hours and nine minutes as the difference, but this is an average figure from which there is considerable variation. Dublin local time was then twenty-five minutes behind London time, which would bring the difference for high water up to two hours and thirty-four minutes. Flamsteed's figure was thus more accurate than Molyneux's.

A few months later Molyneux told Flamsteed that a custom house official whom he had asked to make observations had given him the following information: at the bar (at the entrance to the harbour) high water at the new and full moon was 10.30, at Ringsend (where ships anchored) it was 10.45, at the Custom House (in the city) it was 11. At the quarter moons the corresponding times were, 5, 5.15, and 5.30. Flamsteed accepted the times for the new and full moon, but queried those for the quarters. He did not comment on the point that these times were apparently given as constants, taking no account of variations from month to month. But he thought that Molyneux could well make the observations himself with the help of a good pocket watch.[31] Molyneux had an answer for this: 'were I furnished with a good pocket watch I should not spare the pain of going to our wharfside, though pretty distant from me, to observe the tides for you, but though I purchased about six years ago a very good watch from the king's watchmaker . . . yet through some fault or other, not to be remedied by all the artists in this town, . . . it is very irregular in its motion'. Flamsteed got him a watch, tested it, and sent it to Dublin, where Molyneux found that it promised well.[32] But he does not appear to have made any observations of the tides with its help.

The next thing Flamsteed heard of Dublin tides was three years later when Halley told him he had received a paper from Molyneux on the subject. Flamsteed was taken aback: 'I was in hopes', he wrote to Molyneux, 'if you had done any such thing you would as soon have imparted it to me as to any other'. Molyneux replied that Halley had put some questions to him about the tides and that he had told him no more than he had previously told Flamsteed.[33] Halley, as editor of the *Philosophical Transactions,* published Molyneux's information together with an observation of his own, pointing out that at the quarter moons high water at Dublin was half an hour later than at the full moon, whereas high water at London Bridge at the quarter moons was more than an hour and a half sooner, relative to the moon being at the meridian, 'as may be seen by the accurate tide-tables of Mr Flamsteed'. Halley explained this by the fact that in a river such as the Thames the fresh water is able to drive back the tide sooner at the quarter moons than in the new and full moon, when the tidal impetus is strongest; on the contrary, in the ports on the sea coast such as Dublin high water was later in the less vigorous neap tides than in the swifter spring tides.[34] The reasoning was illogical, and Flamsteed was severe in his criticism. He made much of the point that readers would ascribe the observation to Molyneux and not to Halley. Flamsteed told Molyneux that he had forced Halley 'to own his own brat, for it is as false as unjust and malicious'. Flamsteed argued that the full moon waters receiving the stronger impulse ought to hold out longer than at the quarter moon. If the neap tides were later at Dublin there must be some reason other than that advanced by Halley. He suggested that the narrow channel between Scotland and Ireland might affect the conditions. The reason for his concern was that it might be inferred from the paper that his tide-tables were not applicable to ports on the open sea.

Flamsteed thought that Molyneux should clear himself of responsibility for such a false and unmathematical conclusion as Halley had foisted on him. He might do this in a letter to his brother which could be shown to the president of the Royal Society.[35] Molyneux replied that he had told Halley to send his letter to Flamsteed 'immediately by the penny post', and he was concerned that Halley had not done so. He thought that Flamsteed's argument was very reasonable and that Halley seemed to be in the wrong. However, he himself had not yet seen that number of the *Transactions* and therefore could not enter into the controversy without involving Flamsteed, which he would be reluctant to do. He enclosed a copy of Halley's letter to him, which was similar to the paragraph added by Halley in the *Transactions.* Molyneux was obviously unwilling to enter into the Flamsteed-Halley vendetta and wished to remain on good terms with both men. He told Flamsteed he would gladly think about the Dublin tides if he could get beyond conjecture: 'for so I account all hypotheses that are offered for the solution of the infinite varieties of the flux and reflux of the seas about the world'.[36] Flamsteed replied with further criticisms of Halley, and sent specific queries for Molyneux to answer with the help of some experienced person.

Molyneux gave a conciliatory answer: 'I acknowledge myself indebted to you for your care of my reputation'. He admitted the force of Flamsteed's criticism of Halley but placed so little stress on conjectural assignment of causes that he was ready to forgive Halley. He also said he had received a letter from Halley expressing regret at the breach with Flamsteed, which he seemed anxious to mend. Molyneux was so certain of Flamsteed's good nature and Christian piety that he need only mention the matter for Flamsteed to make a conciliatory move.[37] Flamsteed was not mollified. He regarded the incident as typical of Halley's behaviour ever since he became acquainted with him. An added insult had been that Molyneux's account of the Dublin tides and Halley's observations on it had received pride of place in that number of the *Transactions,* while Flamsteed's catalogue of eclipses had been relegated to the middle pages. Molyneux answered that he had met an experienced sea captain who had been sailing between Dublin and Chester for forty years, and was a good mathematician into the bargain. This captain had told him that he found little difference in the time of high water at Dublin bar relative to the moon's position at new or full moon and at the quarters. The direction and strength of the wind affected the time of high water relative to the moon's position at all times. Flamsteed replied that his information from the Lancashire coast was that the full moon tides ran half an hour longer than at the quarter moon. He was not impressed by the sea captain's opinion: 'seamen are but coarse noters of times'.[38]

That ended the discussion of tides in the correspondence. It was a subject in which Molyneux had consistently shown less interest than had Flamsteed, and the quarrel between Flamsteed and Halley seems to have given Molyneux a distaste for tidal problems.[39]

Flamsteed included ballistics among his many interests and had compiled a table of ranges. This was shown to Molyneux who was engaged with his father on a series of experiments with guns. He criticised Flamsteed's figures and cited Torricelli, whom he was translating 'for his father's use'. He told Flamsteed that he was making experiments with a small mortarpiece and recording his observations. The experiments were made in a field outside the city wall, off Thomas Street to the west of the city. The tradition of these experiments is said to have survived in the name Molyneux Lane, which is still given to a small street in what is now a built-up area. The experiments were not successful and Molyneux asked Flamsteed to tell him of any recent work on ballistics. He had Galileo and Torricelli and Robert Anderson's *The genuine use and effects of the gun* (1674), but he thought the wars must have led Frenchmen to write on the subject 'both mathematically and practically'. He had to rely on Flamsteed's good will 'because I live here in a corner of the world half buried and know but little of what is doing abroad'. A couple of months later he assured Flamsteed that he was persevering in his experiments and hoped to get a mortarpiece a full two diameters deep. In the meantime he was getting a long bow made with which he hoped to make a variety of experiments.[40]

About a year after that he wrote again to Flamsteed describing his experiments with the mortar. He had also got a long gun, and the experiments continued with both. Molyneux was much gratified when the lord lieutenant, the duke of Ormond, visited the yard, watched the mortar and long gun in action, and had a long conversation with him on the subject of artillery and fortification. In the course of the talk there was discussion of the expertise shown by the French in bombing Genoa. Molyneux drew up a paper on the subject which he showed to the master general of the ordnance, Lord Mountjoy, who was so impressed that he showed it to Ormond and suggested that it should be presented to the king.[41] Samuel Molyneux made use of the experiments to write a treatise on gunnery. The full treatise was not published, but he extracted from it a short manual, *Practical problems concerning the doctrine of projects, design'd for great artillery and mortarpieces.* He had this engraved for the use of gunners. It consisted of thirty-nine propositions regarding the elevation and range of different pieces of artillery.[42]

Molyneux continued to be interested in problems of ballistics. He demonstrated an experiment to the Dublin Philosophical Society on the resistance offered by the air to projectiles, and concluded that it was less than writers on the subject had dogmatically asserted.[43] When he was in London on the way to the Continent in 1685 Molyneux had a talk about ballistics with Halley, who gave him a formula for calculating elevations. Molyneux sent it to his father who passed it on to George Tollet. The latter made it the basis for a paper to the Dublin Society which was also read and discussed at the Royal Society.[44] When Halley published his views on ballistics in the *Philosophical Transactions* he sent an extract containing the formula on elevations to Molyneux, who passed the paper to Tollet. The latter misunderstood Halley's meaning and gave Molyneux an elaborate criticism of the proposition, which Molyneux forwarded to Halley. The resulting controversy ended in Tollet admitting his mistake and Molyneux being obliged to patch up relations between him and an aggrieved Halley.[45]

Molyneux never met Newton, but he had the greatest admiration for him and had carefully studied Newton's writings on optics in the *Philosophical Transactions*. In April 1687, while the *Principia* was going through the press, Halley sent him the first part of it, 'what was finished thereof'. In July he replied: 'After the extraordinary character which you give thereof I am obliged no longer to doubt of its worth, and indeed by that cursory perusal I had of so much (for I have not yet had time to sit down close to it) 'tis incomparable'.[46] In December Flamsteed asked Molyneux what his friends thought of the book. He himself had mastered sixty pages, but had only cursorily looked through the rest. Six months later Molyneux replied that he had not had time to settle seriously to the book: 'For I find I must rub up all the little notions I have of conics and the doctrine of ratio, which are half slipped out of my head, before I venture upon it. And I question after all, whether I shall be able to master it, for I perceive it is a piece that requires great application, or else it is invincible. Neither do I know any mathematic head in this place, that has thoroughly considered the whole, unless it be the honourable Mr Robarts, the earl of Radnor's younger son, who is at present in this town. I am very happy sometimes in his company, for he is a most excellent mathematician and admirably accomplish'd otherwise, besides his extraordinary skill in music . . . He tells me he has run through Mr Newton's book and finds it really admirable.'[47] Molyneux made some effort to tackle the *Principia* and referred to parts of it in his *Dioptrica nova*. But there seems no doubt that his mathematical knowledge was insufficient for a fuller understanding of Newton's advocacy of spherical, in preference to conical, lenses: 'But all farther endeavours for forming conic glasses . . . may now be put to a full stop, when we hear in this matter the opinion of as great a philosopher and mathematician as this or any age could ever boast of, the celebrated Mr Newton of Cambridge, who in his profound treatise, *Philosophiae naturalis principia mathematica,* has fathomed the greatest depths of nature and laid a foundation for posterity to raise an infinite structure'.[48] In 1697 Molyneux wrote to Hans Sloane that he had heard that the first edition of the *Principia* was exhausted and that Newton was planning a second edition. He asked Sloane to advise Newton 'to make it a little more plain to readers not so well versed in abstruse mathematics; a few marginal notes and references and quotations would do the business'. He also told Sloane that if Newton was not inclined to include some elucidations in a second edition he might leave the task to others: 'If you know any ingenious mathematician fit for this work that would undertake it he should not want what encouragement I could give him, even from my purse'.[49] At that time Molyneux was closely involved in political questions, but he showed that he had kept some of his early enthusiasm for mathematics, at a level within his grasp.

III

THE DUBLIN PHILOSOPHICAL SOCIETY

IN 1678 Moses Pitt, a London bookseller, launched an ambitious project for an English atlas that was intended to match the great Dutch atlases of Jannson and Blaeu. The project, which was for a work of eleven volumes, with maps and written descriptions of all the countries then known, was submitted to the Royal Society. The concept had a natural appeal for the society, but it failed to realise that Pitt had not the resources, cartographic and financial, to match the Dutch atlases. The scheme was approved and a committee of seven fellows, headed by Sir Christopher Wren, was appointed to supervise it. The committee was later replaced by a board of directors on which Hooke was the most active figure, and finally Hooke acted as sole supervisor.[1]

Molyneux was one of the original subscribers—one of the few from Ireland—and in 1682 he undertook to collect the Irish material for the atlas. He wrote to Flamsteed on 10 June asking for the longitude of London and other places: 'for I must let my worthy friend understand that I am set upon writing the descriptive part of Ireland for the atlas and design to give it to Mr Pitt; for the maps I hope to procure those of Sir William Petty's survey, but his charts want both longitudes and latitudes, which I intend to put to them before they be re-engraved'. It appears that he proposed himself to Pitt, who was presumably satisfied with Molyneux's qualifications for the work. As a preliminary a list of sixteen queries was drawn up. They covered a wide variety of subjects: the soil and its products—animal, vegetable and mineral, rivers and lakes, population, towns trade, history, and 'curiosities of art or nature or antiquity'. The queries were printed in a leaflet which was available *gratis* at a Dublin bookseller's and was presumably also sent to a selection of likely contributors. The answers were to be sent to Molyneux's house 'nigh Ormond's Gate in Dublin', and it was stated that a group of gentlemen in Dublin would meet weekly to examine material submitted by Molyneux. Such meetings were held in Trinity College, and a leading part in them was taken by the provost, Narcissus Marsh, who was himself a subscriber to the English atlas and a notable scholar and bibliophile, devoted to mathematical and scientific pursuits.[2]

Among those whom Molyneux approached for information were his brother-in-law, the younger Sir William Domville, who gave him a description of Queen's County (Laois), and his cousin, Nicholas Dowdall, who supplied an account of Longford.[3] But Molyneux did not confine his inquiries to his own protestant community and showed an unexpected flexibility in seeking out representatives of the other Irish tradition. One of his correspondents was Roderick O'Flaherty, a learned but impoverished antiquary, descended from the Gaelic lords of Connemara. O'Flaherty produced a substantial account of West Connacht, which many years later was published under the title *A chorographical description of West or h-Iar Connaught, written A.D. 1684*.[4] He wrote with enthusiasm of his native region, praising its climate and its richness in natural resources. He gave a lively description of its birds, beasts, and fishes, though his imagination ran away with him in his story of the Irish crocodile in Lough Corrib. His account of the mixed economy, pasture and tillage, and of the painstaking fertilisation and cultivation of unpromising ground is of interest to economic historians. The reader is given an excellent survey of the whole region, and Molyneux had reason to be pleased with this contribution. O'Flaherty's friend and fellow-antiquary, Tadhg O'Roddy, supplied a brief but interesting account of his native Leitrim. He described the inhabitants of the county as 'very much addicted to hospitality, freely mixing and receiving all men into their houses and giving the best fare that they have, which, together with their unthriftiness, renders them poorer than their more retentive neighbours'.[5]

One of the most valuable contributions to Molyneux's collection was the account of Westmeath, written by Sir Henry Piers, a grandson of the learned Sir James Ware. It seems to have been the bishop of the diocese, Molyneux's brother-in-law, Anthony Dopping, who asked Piers to submit an account and then asked him to expand his first effort. The final version was the longest and most comprehensive in the Molyneux collection. It described farming methods and the organisation of the rural economy, marriages, wakes and such festivities as dancing for the cake. In contradistinction to the accounts of O'Flaherty and O'Roddy that of Piers represented the outlook of a well-informed and not unsympathetic protestant landlord. He regretted that the people clung so obstinately to their religion 'in all its gaiety and superstitious forms'; he noted with satisfaction that

English ways and English speech were spreading: 'the people are become more polite and civil'.[6]

In 1683 Moses Pitt came over to Dublin and stayed there for several months. Molyneux arranged with him that there should be five maps in the Irish section, and he told his brother that the maps were being engraved by Sandys. Presumably the maps were of Ireland and of each of the four provinces. Edwin Sandys was a noted Dublin engraver who did the portrait of Petty for his *Hiberniae delineatio* (1685). Molyneux had also an independent plan for a large-scale map of Dublin, six feet by four. However, this plan seems to have collapsed. As he wrote to his brother: 'in my last I gave you some hopes of seeing a map of this place; but workmen and mechanics are so hard to be brought to agree with each other, that I now begin to question whether I shall accomplish my design. The graver and the surveyor do so stand off from what they first proposed'.[7] He was always interested in maps and complained that French and Dutch maps were 'wonderfully erroneous in their longitudes'. He wanted Halley to publish a map of the world, based on astronomical observations, and was sure he would make money by it.[8]

Molyneux drew on the accounts submitted by his correspondents to draft the description of Ireland for the atlas. But his labour was in vain, as the *English atlas* was brought to a sudden halt after four volumes, covering the northern part of continental Europe, had been published. Pitt had got into serious financial difficulties and was arrested on 13 April 1685. Molyneux was disgusted and burned all that he himself had written. Fortunately, he kept communications he had received, hoping that some day the atlas would be continued. Historians have found much valuable material in Molyneux's collection.[9]

Molyneux's correspondence with O'Flaherty about the description of West Connacht led to a lasting friendship and to the development in Molyneux of an interest in early Irish history. He thought O'Flaherty the most learned antiquary that Gaelic Ireland had produced, but too credulous, 'such as suits not a solid historian'. He told his brother that he found O'Flaherty a learned and rational man 'from whose endeavours (if possible) we may expect some light into our profound antiquities'.[10] O'Flaherty's *magnum opus* was *Ogygia, seu rerum Hibernicarum chronologia*. Ogygia as a name for Ireland was not taken from Calypso's island in the Odyssey. It was borrowed, via Camden, from Plutarch's *Voyage to the moon*, where it is described as an island west of Britain. O'Flaherty said that Plutarch's island was a matter of indifference to him. He was more impressed by Camden's observation: 'Ireland is justly called Ogygia, i.e. very ancient, according to Plutarch, for the Irish date their history from the first eras of the world'. *Ogygia* is a learned treatise, compiled from manuscript sources for the shadowy regions of Irish pre-history and early history, with much emphasis on chronology and the synchronising of events in Ireland with those in other parts of the world. The end of the book is almost reached by the time he gets to St Patrick, though a rapid gallop through the centuries enables him to end with an eclipse of the sun on 2 July 1684. One object of the book was to establish the greater antiquity of Irish kings compared with those of Scotland (to whom he gave an Irish origin at the beginning of the sixth century A.D.) and to rebut Scottish claims to greater antiquity. The dedication was to James, duke of York, who was about to become James II, and spoke of Ireland as the most ancient nursery of his ancestors.

O'Flaherty and Molyneux engaged in friendly discussion about the credibility of ancient Irish history, and O'Flaherty in a later letter remarked that he had believed he had satisfied Molyneux's doubts.[11] The doubts were sufficiently allayed for Molyneux to help in getting *Ogygia* published in London. As he wrote to his brother: 'I have in my hands and do suddenly intend to send them over the first part of the *Ogygia*. I think, indeed, 'tis not contemptible, and that is enough to be said of anything relating to the profound antiquities of our country, concerning which little has yet been said that would not raise scorn in a reader'.[12] One of the problems in printing *Ogygia* was that the Latin was punctuated with names and annotations in Irish, for which special type was needed. At this time no Dublin printer had such type. But fortunately a fount of Irish type had been cut in England by Joseph Moxon, at Robert Boyle's expense, and used for the printing in London of the 1681 edition of the *New Testament* in Irish, the printer being Robert Everingham. And it was Everingham who printed *Ogygia*; the publisher was Benjamin Tooke, who had published Descartes's *Meditations* for Molyneux and had become his bookseller and agent. An Irish edition of *Ogygia*, also printed by Everingham, had a different title-page, stating that it was being sold by James Malone, who was a catholic bookseller in Dublin.

Ogygia was a substantial and significant book, which set a new level in the treatment of early Irish history. O'Flaherty combined a passion for accuracy with a thorough knowledge of Irish and classical sources. The book bristles with the apparatus of scholarship and is patently the work of a learned man. His rebuttal of Scottish claims for the antiquity of their monarchy involved O'Flaherty in a controversy already going on between a Scots controversialist, Sir George Mackenzie, and English bishops. Mackenzie at once added O'Flaherty to the objects of his castigation. But elsewhere *Ogygia* was treated as a standard work throughout the eighteenth century, and by making its publication possible Molyneux rendered a service to Irish historiography. More modern comment has varied between admiration for O'Flaherty's industry and scholarship, and criticism of his theorising. A recent verdict is that '*Ogygia* is the most learned exposition of Gaelic loyalty to the Stuart cause and to the concept of the kingdom of Ireland'.[13] The latter element, but not the former, had a strong appeal for Molyneux. Among his papers are a manuscript copy of 'Ogygia', and two manuscripts written in English by O'Flaherty: a chronology of Irish and Scottish kings and a tract, 'St Columba vindicated'.

It is remarkable that Molyneux should have established such friendly relations with the catholic antiquary, living Irish-style in remote Connemara, absorbed in legends of the Gaelic past. But there were several precedents for friendship on an intellectual basis between protestants and catholics: scholarship was an effective breaker of barriers. O'Flaherty's devotion to learning was a triumph of mind over adversity. He had been left with only a fraction of his former estate and had great difficulty in making ends meet. Molyneux persuaded his brother-in-law, 'the good bishop of Meath', to give some financial support to O'Flaherty, but this ended with the bishop's death. O'Flaherty's last letter to Molyneux, in 1697, was written from Galway gaol.[14] The friendship was continued by Molyneux's son Samuel, who visited O'Flaherty in 1709 and found him very old and in a miserable condition: 'his ill fortune had stripped him of [his Irish manuscripts] as well as his other goods'.[15]

In October 1683, while the work of collecting material for the atlas was in progress, Molyneux set himself to form a society in Dublin 'agreeable to the design of the Royal Society'. He claimed that he was the first to take up the project, being assisted in the task by St George Ashe, his college contemporary, who was by now a fellow of the college. It seems probable that the work on the atlas, and in particular the weekly meetings to consider progress, suggested to him that this would be a suitable opportunity to establish such a society. The response to his search for materials had been such as to suggest that Ireland offered an ample field for philosophical inquiry of every kind. By this time also there had emerged a group interested in the mathematical sciences and capable of making a significant contribution to them. Molyneux's decision may well have been stimulated by his brother's letters describing his visits to the Royal Society and his impression of individual members.

To begin with, there was no regular constitution, and meetings took place in an informal way. Molyneux referred to the group as 'the rudiments of a society, for which I have drawn up rules, and called it *conventio philosophica*'.[16] They were encouraged by a cordial letter from Dr Plot, secretary of both the Royal Society and the Oxford Society, assuring them that both societies would welcome the establishment of a similar society in Dublin.[17] A committee, including Molyneux and Petty, was appointed to draft a constitution, which was to be read at three meetings before it was adopted. Under the rules each member on admission had to subscribe an 'obligation' to promote the aims of the society. There were fourteen original subscribers, including Molyneux himself, Petty, Narcissus Marsh, lately provost of the college, Robert Huntington, his successor, and the mathematicians George Tollet and St George Ashe. A Dublin doctor, Charles Willoughby, was chosen to be the first director (the term initially adopted). Molyneux became secretary and treasurer. He conducted the correspondence with Plot and with Aston, who succeeded Plot as a secretary of the Royal Society. Molyneux was deeply touched by Plot referring to him as 'dear brother' and addressed him in the same terms. The minutes of the Dublin Society were regularly sent to the Royal Society and by it communicated to the Oxford Society. Those societies in turn sent their minutes to Dublin.

The establishment of the Dublin Society seems to have involved more tension than appears from the euphoric correspondence. Molyneux wrote to his brother in Holland: 'how I have laboured to bring it [the society] to what it is I will not say; it would be a surprising relation to you to hear the several passages I have run through, but these I keep till I see you.' One subject of tension may have been the selection of the director. It was surprising that Petty, much the most celebrated member, should not have been chosen. And when the title was changed to president at the end of the year Petty was elected only on the second count after a tie with Willoughby. But much progress was made during 1684, the first year of the society. Thirty-eight meetings were held, and at the end of the year there were thirty-three members. However, Molyneux was conscious of the difficulty of keeping up the impetus with which the society had begun. He told his brother: 'we'll go as far as we can; and if we can go no farther but grow weak, decay and die we are but *in statu quo prius*'.[18] To Flamsteed he wrote on 8 April 1684: 'we have begun (I dare not say settled) a weekly meeting for philosophical and mathematical knowledge, but that we should have stock enough to continue it I dare not promise, for indeed this city is not yet sufficiently replenished with men that way inclined ... but this I write through diffidence of ourselves, not that I have any certain prospect of our failure'. In May 1684 Molyneux was able to tell his brother: 'our society goes on; we have a fair room in Crow's-nest ... where we have a fair garden for plants, and a laboratory erected for us'.[19] Crow's Nest was a house built in 1597 by an official named William Crow. In 1684 it belonged to an apothecary from whom the Philosophical Society hired rooms. Crow Street still commemorates the builder of the house.[20] He later asked his brother to take good note of the design of Dutch laboratories, as he hoped that 'we shall be the erectors and masters of as good a laboratory as can be desired for all chemical and philosophical operations, together with a convenient place for dissection and astronomical observations; therefore I would have you acquaint yourself well therein, that when we come to the work we may not be strangers to it.'[21]

Molyneux was on very friendly terms with Petty, and also with Lord Mountjoy, master-general of the ordnance, who succeeded Petty as president. He gave up the treasurership at the end of 1684, but continued as secretary until he left for the Continent in May 1685, his place being taken by Ashe. When Molyneux returned to Dublin in the autumn he was elected to the council of the society and continued to take an active part in its work, as is evident from the frequent mention of his name in the minutes. The first phase of the society continued up to 11 April 1687, after which the anxiety caused to the protestant community by Lord Tyrconnell's style of government made the members disinclined for philosophical discussions.

During this first phase Molyneux discoursed to the society on twenty different subjects. Nine of his papers were subsequently published in the *Philosophical Transactions* of the Royal Society. The subjects were extraordinarily varied, including optics, astronomy, the identification of a caterpillar, the dissection of a newt, and the allegedly petrifying qualities of Lough Neagh. In an age of versatile virtuosi Molyneux was more versatile than most. He was particularly proud of his feat in dissecting the newt, and repeated his demonstration more than once. The minutes of the society record that with the help of a microscope he showed the circulation of the blood 'as plainly as water running in a river and more rapidly than any common stream'.[22] He wrote to his brother: 'I have shown before our society the dissection of newts this summer, and the

wonderful circulation of the blood, it makes some discourse about the town as admirable; and yet our perverse Irish physicians impute it to the agonies the creature is in by being laid open.'[23] It was gratifying to be able to report his achievement to a medical student. Two years later he was disconcerted to find that Dr George Garden, an Aberdeen divine, had written to the Royal Society about his own observation of the circulation of blood in a newt. Molyneux protested and sent the society an account of his experiment, supported by an extract from the minutes of the Dublin Society. The Royal Society concluded that Molyneux should be given the credit unless Dr Garden could produce evidence to the contrary, which he failed to do. Molyneux's paper was then published in the *Philosophical Transactions*.[24]

The petrifying qualities of Lough Neagh were the subject of much interest to the societies in Dublin, London, and Oxford. Attention had been drawn to the phenomenon in Boate's *Ireland's naturall history* (1652), in which it was discussed at some length, with the conclusion that there was at any rate a general belief that wood put into the lough, particularly into certain parts of it, would become petrified. Verses in O'Flaherty's *Ogygia,* based on old Irish sources dealing with the wonders of Ireland, also told of this phenomenon. They described how a branch of holly immersed in Lough Neagh for seven years would turn into stone, while the part embedded in the lake floor would become iron. Soon after the Dublin Society was established, the Oxford Society was shown a specimen of 'Lough Neagh stone, originally holly', and it was decided to ask the Dublin Society for their views. Molyneux promptly produced a paper, in which he said it was generally agreed by the inhabitants of the area that Lough Neagh had the power of petrifying holly, but no other wood. His estimate of local opinion no doubt came from the Molyneux estate of Castle Dillon, which is not far from Lough Neagh. He rejected the opinion of a local gentleman who had written to him to deny the petrifying power of the water, on the ground that an oak stake had failed to become petrified. Molyneux had himself examined a specimen of petrified wood and found it to be 'perfectly of the colour and grain of holly'. His paper was read to the Dublin Society and then sent to the Oxford Society, which ordered that thanks be returned to Mr Molyneux for his ingenious discourse and that he be asked to answer some further questions. The paper was also printed in the *Philosophical Transactions*.[25]

Some months later Molyneux read another paper to the Dublin Society, in which he propounded ten queries about Lough Neagh. This was an advance on the somewhat uncritical spirit he had shown in his original discourse. He now asked whether Lough Neagh really had the power of petrifying, and whether anyone had tested it by experiment. His queries were handed over to Edward Smyth, a fellow of Trinity College and a member of the Dublin Society, who originally came from the neighbourhood of Lough Neagh and now intended to visit it. Smyth consulted Arthur Brownlow, an enlightened landlord in Lurgan, who drew up a series of replies to the queries. Brownlow said that the experiment of putting holly sticks into the water had proved negative. He thought that the water had no petrifying power, but that the mud had such power, over oak and not alone holly. This paper, which was in effect a contradiction of Molyneux's, was also published in the *Philosophical Transactions*.[26] Specimens of silicified wood have in fact been found on the shores of Lough Neagh, but modern opinion is that the silicification took place a very long time ago, in tertiary times. There is no evidence that wood, whether holly or otherwise, that is now put into the lough will become silicified. Halley had asked Molyneux whether the petrified wood was magnetic. To begin with, Molyneux could discover no magnetic reaction, no matter what he did: he applied a 'large and well-touched needle', he tried putting iron filings on it, and heating it by rubbing. So he pronounced that the stone was not magnetic. Later he changed his mind. His 'ingenious retraction' explained that, when well calcined, 'Lough Neagh stone responded most briskly to the magnet'. This could be accounted for on the assumption that there were traces of iron in the silicate.[27]

There was more scepticism in Molyneux's account of the 'Connough [Connacht] worm which is reported to be the only poisonous animal in our kingdom'. In his account of Westmeath Sir Edward Piers had given an alarming account of the horrors of this creature—'many short feet, a large head, great goggle eyes and glaring . . . whatever beast happeneth to feed where this venemous worm hath crept . . . is certainly poisoned'.[28] Molyneux asked his cousin, Nicholas Dowdall, if he could produce a specimen. Two years later Dowdall replied: 'I have by much search found out at last the Connough worm'.[29] It was sent up to Dublin on a grassy sod, but arrived in such a poor condition that Molyneux stifled it with sulphur. His account of it, which was read out both to the Oxford Society and the Royal Society, described a series of popular beliefs about the 'worm', but came to the correct conclusion that it was an elephant caterpillar, of which he had seen an illustration in a recent book on insects. Molyneux's account was published in the *Philosophical Transactions* and, translated into Latin, got as far as Leipzig, where it was published in the *Acta Eruditorum*.[30] As a contribution to a learned journal it has an air of naivety. But this was not unusual in the material published in the *Philosophical Transactions*. Molyneux did not write it as a formal article, but as a letter to a secretary of the Royal Society, in which he made the most of the adventures of a caterpillar. This was, by the standards of the day, quite acceptable for publication.

The minutes of the Dublin Society show that, apart from his discourses, Molyneux took a very active part in the proceedings, demonstrating experiments, discussing books, showing curious objects. When the society ordered that an eclipse of the sun, expected on 2 July 1684, should be 'calculated from the best modern tables and observed accordingly', Molyneux and Ashe undertook the task. Unfortunately the day was overcast and they could take only fleeting observations. Molyneux also undertook to calculate and observe the eclipse of the moon, expected on 11 December 1684, but he was even more unfortunate with that as the sky was completely overcast and no observations could be made.[31]

The society was concerned that regular weather records should be maintained. Petty thought that it would be very difficult to do this properly without a great apparatus of instruments. But Molyneux undertook to record the weather by means of a baroscope, as recommended by Martin Lister. He explained his method in a letter to his brother: each day he marked the height of the mercury, the direction and strength of the wind, and at bedtime wrote a brief note of the day's weather. He had his weather diary for May 1684 engraved and sent copies to the Royal Society for distribution to other weather observers. He particularly asked that copies should be sent to Oxford, 'for we are in their debt'. A sample has been preserved at Oxford.[32] He continued to keep his weather diary until the following spring, when he left for the Continent and Ashe took on the responsibility. Subsequently, in 1686, he reported to the society his comparison of the weather at Oxford and at Dublin, at both of which similar day-to-day variations in the mercury level were recorded, though the Dublin levels tended to be higher. Sudden changes in the weather took place at the same time in both places. His conclusion was that Dublin enjoyed as much good weather as Oxford.[33]

One of the devices for weather forecasting developed by Hooke was a hygroscope for measuring the humidity of the air. Hooke's instrument made use of a straw of a wild oat. Molyneux found that the oat straw grew weak in time and that a more durable material was required. He devised a hygroscope of whipcord, which twisted and untwisted with changes in humidity. A weight was fixed to the cord and carried a pointer which moved over a graduated dial. A description of the 'Dublin hygroscope' was published in the *Philosophical Transactions* and also in the *Acta Eruditorum* of Leipzig.[34] The latter pointed out that Molyneux's idea had been thought of already. He later admitted this, but said he had not been aware of it at the time that he demonstrated his hygroscope to the Dublin Society. Bishop Narcissus Marsh suggested to the society that an improvement could be made on Molyneux's whipcord by the use of a lute string.[35]

Experiment was an essential part of the new style of philosophical inquiry, and the Dublin Society engaged in a number of experiments, some of them hazardous. Petty was an indefatigable seeker after new forms of transport, both by land and by water. His original double-bottom (i.e. twin-hulled boat), *The Experiment,* had foundered in the Irish Sea during a storm, but it was followed by later models. In 1684 Molyneux and thirteen others each subscribed £20 to build *St Michael the Archangel*. Petty was confident that this double-bottom would be successful, but the cautious Pepys wagered Petty that *St Michael* would not stand the test.[36] In the event Pepys was proved right, and Molyneux had an unhappy story to give the Royal Society of her trial run in Dublin harbour: 'she performed so abominably, as if built on purpose to disappoint . . . the wind did but just fill her sails and yet she stooped, so that she was in danger of being overset every moment; a blast from a smith's bellows superadded had overturned her . . . The seamen swear they would not venture over the bar with her for £1000 apiece.'[37] Among the varieties of land transport in which Petty was interested was a calash (a low-wheeled light carriage) specially designed for rough cross-country journeys. He and Molyneux spent a day driving over ploughed fields, irregular banks, and ditches. The vehicle tilted alarmingly but always righted itself.[38] One of Molyneux's more dangerous experiments was with *pulvis fulminans,* a fearsome compound of nitre, sulphur, and tartar. On the instructions of the society he charged a pistol with the mixture, thrust the breech through the bars of a hot fire, and pointed the mouth of the loaded barrel at a post in front of it. By good fortune the weapon did not burst, and the bullet penetrated the post in the same way as if gunpowder had been used.[39]

After the Irish war of 1689-91 had ended in the defeat of the Jacobites and the re-establishment of the protestant ascendancy, the Dublin Society revived. The opening meeting of the second phase of the society was held on 26 April 1693. Molyneux was present with four others of the pre-war members: St George Ashe (now provost of the College), Narcissus Marsh (now archbishop of Cashel), Dr Willoughby (director in the society's first year), and Sir Cyril Wyche, an ex-president of the Royal Society who had joined the Dublin Society when he was Ormond's secretary and was now one of the lords justices who administered the government of Ireland; he became president of the society at the end of 1693. The meeting was held in the provost's lodgings, and notice was ordered to be given to former members that weekly meetings would take place there. By 1694 there were fifty-one members. Molyneux did not hold office in the revived society, and as minutes were not regularly kept it is difficult to judge how much part he took in the proceedings. There are minutes for the first three meetings held in 1693, at all of which he was present. During the second and third meetings there was a discussion, in which Molyneux took an active part, about a natural history of Ireland. It appears to have been in connection with this history that the society drew up an elaborate questionnaire covering such topics as climate, stones, metals, husbandry, and antiquities. It was entitled 'Enquiries to be propounded to the most ingenious of each county in Ireland in order to the history of nature and the arts'. Copies were printed for distribution, but we have no evidence of the response.[40] The society hoped to induce Edward Lhuyd, the well-known Welsh antiquary, to come to Ireland and undertake this history. Lhuyd had visited Dublin before the war and had then met members of the society.[41] But the society was unable to offer him enough money to lure him from Oxford, where he was keeper of the Ashmolean Museum. Sixty pounds per annum would have attracted him, but there was no prospect of his getting so much. So Molyneux regretfully agreed that they must do without Lhuyd, to whom he wrote: 'we must be content to want your desirable company in this country'.[42] Some years later, Samuel Molyneux, William's son, drew up a scheme for a natural history, but never got beyond the preliminaries.[43]

After the early meetings of 1693 until the society again faded out about the end of 1697 there is no direct evidence of Molyneux's participation in the meetings, and his growing involvement with politics distracted him from natural philosophy. However, he did not abandon his interest in scientific questions, and it is likely, for instance, that his paper on the effect of magnetic variation on surveys, which was published in the *Philosophical Transactions* in 1697, was previously read to the Dublin Society.[44] From a letter of the secretary of the Dublin Society, written in 1694, it appears that there was a project to draw up lists of natural objects for England and Ireland, in which Molyneux undertook to deal with birds, but there is no evidence that he did so.[45] He also took an interest in the investigation of the Giant's Causeway, which was a continuing pre-occupation of the Dublin Society at this time.[46]

Molyneux's doubts whether Dublin was sufficiently supplied with inquirers after knowledge to sustain a lasting society were proved to be well founded. The original impetus was largely provided by his inspiration and energy, and maintained for four years by the efforts of himself, Ashe, and a nucleus of able enthusiasts. What brought that phase to an end was the tension created by the policies of the Jacobite government. The post-war revival had less promise of endurance, and Molyneux had other preoccupations that made him devote less energy to the society. The revival that his son Samuel initiated in 1707 brought in a distinguished new member in George Berkeley and produced some valuable papers. But this third phase of the society was short-lived, lasting less than a year, and while it lasted depended greatly on the individual efforts of Samuel, its secretary.[47] However, though the Dublin Philosophical Society had a chequered life it was the forerunner of what became the Royal Dublin Society, of which Thomas Molyneux was a founder member in 1731, and which his, and William's, nephew 'Premium' Madden did much to set on a firm course. This Dublin Society developed the more utilitarian aspects of its predecessor. It was followed in 1786 by the Royal Irish Academy with its emphasis on scientific and antiquarian inquiry. The Dublin Philosophical Society was an experiment in the collective pursuit of learning in many fields, and William Molyneux, supported by his brother Thomas and followed by his son Samuel, made a genuine contribution to the advancement of learning in Ireland.

IV

BROTHERS ABROAD

IN May 1683 Thomas Molyneux, who was then twenty-two and
had taken his bachelor's degree at Trinity College, Dublin, left
for further medical studies at Leyden, the most celebrated school
of medicine in protestant Europe. The parting was a wrench for
William. The two brothers were united by much affection and by
similar interests in knowledge of every kind. Copies have been preserved of their correspondence during Thomas's absence.[1] The
letters throw much light on their personalities and on the impact
that contact with Europe had on them. The day after Thomas had
sailed William wrote: 'I have no one now with me that takes delight
in the subjects I fancy, or with whom I can exchange a thought
concerning a book'.[2] Evidently even so intelligent a father as Samuel
was no substitute for a brother. William begged Thomas to write
constantly and tell him of all the impressions he formed: William
would keep the letters and save Thomas the trouble of keeping a
diary. Thomas responded faithfully and gave William a full account
of his travels from the time he reached England.

William had given Thomas letters of introduction to several
members of the Royal Society. One of them was Flamsteed, and
Thomas went down to Greenwich observatory to call on him. Un-
luckily Flamsteed was away, but his assistant showed Thomas the
instruments and let him look round the premises. On his way back
to London Thomas met Flamsteed at the Tower quay and they
arranged to meet again. He found Flamsteed 'a free, affable, and
humble man, not at all conceited or dogmatical'—a more benevolent
judgment than was usually made about a prickly and inhibited
personality. Other members of the Royal Society whom Thomas met
were Petty, Boyle, Haak and Halley. He was allowed to sit in at a
meeting of the society and was shown over its 'repository'. He had
much talk with Halley, who asked him how William's astronomical
studies were progressing. He had no conversation with Hooke, but
was told he was the most ill-natured, self-conceited man in the
world.[3]

Thomas spent more than two months in England and visited
Oxford and Cambridge, which he described to William in great

detail. At Oxford he stayed in the same house as Edward Bernard, the professor of astronomy, who promised to give him introductions to professors at Leyden. Thomas thought Bernard very slovenly, peevish, ill-natured, and more interested in history and theology than in astronomy. But he made a point of keeping on good terms with him for the sake of the Leyden introductions. He had an introduction to Dr Plot, who showed him over the new Ashmolean Museum and was very cordial and obliging. His description of Cambridge was mainly an account of the colleges, and he did not mention Newton.

Thomas reached Leyden at the end of July and found lodgings in a widow's house. In the autumn he enrolled at the university, which he described to William in a long letter. He was well pleased with his choice: he had 'pretty good information about the state of the other famous universities of the world . . . and I am satisfied this exceeds them all for advantages in the study of physic'. There were sixteen professors, five being professors of medicine whom he named, describing two of them as Cartesians. There were 700 or 800 students, of many nationalities. The professors did not insist on attendance at lectures or classes, so that for young students it was the worst university in the world: but 'for those of riper years . . . (especially for my own faculty) it is one of the best societies in Europe'.[4] In philosophy there were two professors: Senguerdus, an anti-Cartesian whose book Thomas sent to William, and de Volder, a strict Cartesian and an experimental philosopher, who was also professor of mathematics and astronomy. William asked his brother to send him books on optics, and was specially anxious to get one by Huygens. Thomas could hear nothing of that, and said that Huygens had been in France for the last two years. But he hoped to visit Leeuwenhoek at Delft.

William was planning to visit his brother in the summer of 1684, but Thomas warned him not to come, as there was fighting with the French in Flanders. Besides it would be better to wait until Thomas was more settled in and had a good command of Dutch. He evidently thought a visit from William would be too much of an interruption to his work at that stage: 'I am but just settled to my study here, and should I go now and ramble about four or five months more, above a whole year of my life would pass over my head in which I have done nothing'. A further argument that Thomas advanced was that William should not leave Ireland while the Dublin Society was in its infancy: 'certainly in your absence it would come to nought, whereas if it be kept up for a while . . . it may in time, for ought I know become as famous as any whatever in Europe'. Then there was their father to be considered: he should not be 'so suddenly robbed of the conversation and enjoyment of both his sons together'.[5]

Huygens returned to The Hague in the summer of 1684, and Thomas went there to see him. Huygens gave him a very friendly reception and showed him his instruments, including a dial of his own invention which indicated 'the minute, hour, day of the month and year, with the exact postures and aspects that all the planets bear to the sun at that very moment'.[6] He then took Thomas into his garden and demonstrated his contrivance for making a telescope without a tube. He had described this in *Astroscopia compendiaria tubi optici molimine liberata* (The Hague, 1684). Thomas sent the book to William, who showed it to the Dublin Philosophical Society and explained Huygens's method. Thomas's long letter to William about his visit to Huygens was also read to the society. Thomas had described Huygens as a man of about fifty, which puzzled William. He could hardly believe that this was the same Huygens who had invented pendulum clocks and was the author of *Horologium*, published in 1658. Thomas assured him that there was only one Christiaan Huygens. In fact Huygens was fifty-five at this time, and his authorship of *Horologium* was not as precocious as William supposed.

Thomas combined his medical studies at Leyden with an interest in several branches of natural philosophy. He tried to match William's Dublin weather-diary with a diary of Leyden weather, which he sent to William with an apologetic explanation that his observations were useless for lack of a barometer (which seemed to be unheard of in Holland) or a thermometer. He also undertook to obtain for the Royal Society a catalogue of the oriental collection of Dr Paul Hermann, the professor of botany at Leyden. When Thomas arrived there he had brought letters of introduction to Hermann, and had told William how civilly Hermann had received him and shown him his collection of exotic rarities. Thomas sent a full list of the collection to the Royal Society, where it was read.[7] He also visited a similar collection in Amsterdam, assembled by Swammerdam, but failed to get a catalogue of its contents. He sent the Royal Society an account of a 'prodigious *os frontis*' in the Leyden medical school, which was published in the *Philosophical Transactions*.[8]

A controversy, in which both brothers took part, related to the problem of why heavy bodies could be dissolved by solvents lighter than themselves, which seemed to contradict the laws of hydrostatics. Thomas sent a paper on the subject to the celebrated Pierre Bayle. With it he sent a letter to Bayle, telling him how much he admired his *Nouvelles de la république des lettres,* but suggesting that it would be even more admirable if it gave more space to problems of natural philosophy, which were of such interest to contemporaries and filled a great part of other learned journals.[9] Thomas told William that Bayle 'was pleased, after the French way, to commend [the paper] with a great deal of compliment, and publish [it] in his [issue] of August last, and also promised me he would for the future take care to insert as many observations of this nature as he could gather by the help of his correspondents'.[10] In his paper Thomas used the term 'menstrua' which was a borrowing from the vocabulary of alchemists and was in current usage among chemists for any substance that had the power of dissolving another substance. He gave the example of mercury being dissolved by nitric acid which was one-tenth of its density. He accounted for the phenomenon by the argument that liquid which appeared to be static was in fact composed of minute particles in constant motion, which was strong enough to agitate the particles of the heavier substance and allow the process of dissolution to take place.

Bayle's introductory note stated that he had received an explanation of a phenomenon 'worthy of the curiosity of honest men'. He gladly published this explanation, which was extremely probable and intelligible even to the non-specialist. However, he offered an alternative explanation, that the particles of the lighter substance surrounded the heavier particles and carried them upwards. He gave the example of iron nails coated with wax, which would float even though iron by itself would sink.[11] Thomas rebutted Bayles' explanation in another letter, in which he argued that the reason why nails stuck into wax floated was that the composite result was lighter than the surrounding fluid. He added a reinforcement of his original explanation: when a solvent was placed over a 'digestive fire' it was able to dissolve a greater quantity than if it were cold, because the motion of the fluid was more rapid.[12] Bayle published the substance of this letter in his *Nouvelles* for January 1685.[13]

Thomas proudly told his brother of these publications, and William was delighted at this glory, which he presumed to be reflected on Dublin and Ireland, as well as on the Molyneux family: 'the tidings that our name is in the journals of Amsterdam, was very pleasing to me, and really, without vanity, I think our city and nation may be herein something beholding to us, for I believe the name Dublin has hardly ever before been printed or heard of amongst foreigners on a learned account'.[14] In fact, the *Nouvelles* gave no credit to the names of Molyneux or of Dublin and Ireland. It was merely stated that the communication had been received from an Englishman, a good philosopher as were many of that 'ingenious nation'.

When William studied Thomas's papers he disagreed with his arguments and joined in the debate with a paper published in the *Philosophical Transactions,* which began with a justification of brother biting brother: 'The liberty of philosophising being now universally granted between all men, I am sure that a difference of opinion will be no breach of affection between two entirely loving brothers'. William argued that the accepted law of hydrostatics, that a heavier body in a lighter fluid will sink, was defective and did not allow for the resistance of the fluid. As the resistance of the air made Galileo's formula inapplicable to small particles so the resistance of the fluid would keep afloat small particles of substances whose specific gravity was greater. The *Philosophical Transactions* include a postscript by Thomas, admitting the factor of resistance but maintaining that his own explanation held good: resistance might keep a particle from sinking, but could never in the first instance account for its rising from the bottom.[15]

In the autumn of 1683 John Locke found it advisable to withdraw from an England in which whigs were objects of hostility and the king had shaken off the incubus of parliament. He found asylum in Holland and in October 1684 spent about a month at Leyden, where he found pleasure in conversations with Thomas Molyneux. When Locke moved on to Utrecht he wrote a cordial letter to Thomas saying he often wished he were back in Leyden, 'having not passed any of my time on this side the water so pleasantly as there, for which I am indebted to the civility of those gentlemen I had the honour to converse with there, and particularly to yours'.[16] He asked Thomas to look for some papers that he thought he had left behind in his lodging, directions for the treatment of a child of between two and three years old—evidently the son of his friend, Edward Clarke. Some years later, when Locke began his correspondence with William, he asked him whether the Molyneux he had known in Leyden was related to him. William replied that Locke's Leyden acquaintance was his brother, and enclosed a letter from Thomas. Locke then wrote to Thomas saying that he had often thought of him and regretted that distance allowed him no hope of renewing the acquaintance: 'there being nothing that I think of so much value as the acquaintance and friendship of knowing and worthy men.'[17]

Not content with his work for the Dublin Philosophical Society William Molyneux set about securing an official appointment. The holder of the post of surveyor-general and chief engineer in Ireland was William Robinson, who was in the process of completing his great work at the Royal Hospital, Kilmainham, on the outskirts of Dublin, designed as a resting-place for retired soldiers of the army

in Ireland. It is still one of Dublin's most impressive buildings and
the only major architectural work of the seventeenth century.
Molyneux greatly admired it: as he told his brother "tis a most
stately, beautiful piece of building perhaps as Christendom affords
for that use'.[18] Robinson had a patent for life for his appointment,
which carried an annual salary of £300. Molyneux offered him a
lump sum of £250 to exchange this patent for one to himself and
Molyneux jointly, the longer liver of the two (which turned out to
be Robinson) to get the sole appointment. Robinson agreed and
government approval of the arrangement was readily forthcoming,
thanks to Ormond's high opinion of Molyneux. The new patent
was granted on 31 October 1684, a few months before Ormond's
viceroyalty was brought to an end at the beginning of James II's
reign.[19] In February 1687 when Lord Clarendon, after little more
than a year as viceroy, was replaced by the catholic Lord Tyrconnell
Robinson decided to repair to England, leaving Molyneux in sole
charge. The major work then in hand was the restoration of Dublin
Castle, badly damaged by a fire in April 1684, which, as Molyneux
told his brother, 'destroyed all the lodgings and rooms of state,
with a vast deal of goods and furniture'.[20] There must have been
some repair done by the time Clarendon arrived in January 1686,
but he complained that it was 'the worst lodging a gentleman ever
lay in'.[21] The major reconstruction was left for Molyneux to execute,
and he told his brother that in the eighteen months between
Robinson's departure and his own dismissal by Tyrconnell he built
'the great new building on piers and arches that runs along the
south wall of the castle, with the terrace walk behind it'.[22] This
disappeared when Dublin Castle was reconstructed in the eighteenth
century. But a description by John Dunton, a travelling bookseller
with a gift for observation, who visited Ireland in 1698, gives some
idea of the work: 'The building is handsome without much mag-
nificence on the outside; you enter the house up a noble stairs and
find several stately rooms, one of which is called the presence
chamber and has a chair of state with a canopy over it. One part of
the house stands over a large stone gallery supported by several
pillars of stone. At the back of the house lies a broad terrace walk
. . . from hence on a stone arch over a little river you descend by
two spacious pair of stone stairs.'[23] A set of drawings among the
King's Maps in the British Library appears to be the designs for
this building. The use of arcades is very like that in the Royal
Hospital, and it is probable that the designs are Robinson's and
that Molyneux was responsible only for the execution.[24]

William's journey to the Continent was made in the summer of

1685. Just before he left Dublin his wife gave birth to a son named William, not for his father, but for his grandfather, Sir William Domville. In spite of her poor constitution Lucy recovered well and the child appeared quite healthy. He could therefore set out on his travels with a good conscience. His journey was given an official stamp by a grant of £100 from the Irish government to enable him to inspect fortresses in the Netherlands. The grant had been promised by Ormond before he gave up the viceroyalty. The ostensible object was 'for qualifying him the better for his majesty's service'.[25] But there was something of a 'fiddle' about the arrangement as it was agreed with Lord Mountjoy, the master general of the ordnance, that Molyneux should provide companionship to Robert Stewart (Mountjoy's son), who was already in France.

William left Dublin on 13 May 1685, crossed England, and got a packet boat at Dover for Calais, which he reached on 6/16 June. Robert Stewart met him there and accompanied him throughout his continental travels. They reached Leyden on 25 June/5 July, and after that Thomas joined them on a three-month tour which covered the Netherlands and parts of Germany, and wound up in Paris, where William left Thomas and Stewart and returned homeward via Calais. There is no continuous record of their travels, nothing beyond scattered references to persons met and things observed. They visited Huygens at The Hague, when he showed them an arrangement of lenses in his garden and his planetary clock, 'a machine that cannot be sufficiently admired'.[26] When they visited Leeuwenhoek in Delft he showed several microscopes, but was reluctant to bring out his best ones. Thomas had paid an earlier visit to Leeuwenhoek and had the same experience, but he was impressed by the quality of the instruments he was allowed to see.[27] When they crossed the Rhine at Cologne William admired the clever use of the current to move the large double-bottomed ferry along a rope stretched across the river. He described the process to the Dublin Philosophical Society when he got home. At a subsequent meeting he described a similar method used at Utrecht.[28] There is no indication that he made any inspection of fortifications in the Netherlands, the ostensible object of his journey. In Paris they visited the astronomer Jean-Dominique Cassini, to whom Flamsteed had given William an introduction. At the observatory, of which he was the first director, he showed a clockwork device for keeping a heavenly body covered by the object glass of a telescope. He also showed how he tested his lenses by fixing a book open at the title page, to the window of a church steeple more than a quarter of a mile away.[29] He also met 'Mons. Borelly', apparently Pierre Borel, a prominent doctor who had written about telescopes and microscopes, whom he found to be 'a person of the greatest candour and freedom and the most communicative'. Borel gave him an object glass designed for a twenty-four foot telescope.[30]

Molyneux reached London on 5 September 1685, and spent two or three weeks there before returning home. Flamsteed heard of his arrival and sent him a cordial invitation to visit him at Greenwich and talk about his travels, 'if your occasions will permit to make a little voyage to Greenwich and stay a night or two with me. You will find clean linen, slender fare, and hearty welcome . . . If you bring no company besides your servant our conversation will be the freer.'[31] It was unfortunate that Molyneux did not do as Flamsteed requested. He allowed Halley to come with him. Flamsteed, who had formed an intense dislike of Halley (whom he suspected of intriguing to supplant him) was highly indignant: 'I plainly told him before he thrust himself upon you as a companion hither that I would make no provision for him'. The visit was evidently a very uncomfortable affair and was the source of much malicious gossip about Flamsteed: 'having invited some friends down to Greenwich he treated them with cold coast of lamb'. Flamsteed was very upset about the incident, but seems to have blamed Halley rather than Molyneux. He kept referring to the subject and was obsessed with the idea that Halley and his friends were defaming him. His bitter feelings were revealed by the violence of his expressions: 'They are an odd sort of people that are not to be esteemed Christians, and a modest heathen would be ashamed of their way. That creed is theirs which serves their interest best, and such cattle are dangerous.'[32] Halley had the reputation of being opposed to Christianity and has been identified as the 'infidel mathematician' to whom Berkeley addressed the *Analyst*.[33] A more agreeable side to Molyneux's visit was his account of the instruments used by French astronomers. They were scarcely half the radius of those used by Flamsteed and much less adapted to their purpose.[34]

Molyneux's stay in London gave him the opportunity of employing a celebrated instrument-maker, Richard Whitehead, to make a combined dial and telescope to Molyneux's own design. This instrument to which he gave the name *Sciothericum telescopicum* (from the Greek work for sundial) was something of a disappointment, though he evidently took considerable pride in it: a poor thing but his own. Before despatching the *Sciothericum* to Dublin Whitehead took it down to Greenwich to show to Flamsteed, who seems not to have been impressed. He advised Molyneux to try it on two stars well separated, a test it apparently failed to pass to Flamsteed's satisfaction. Molyneux protested that the instrument had not then been properly adjusted, but he confessed that the structure of the telescope was not strong enough and that this led to inaccuracy, though he had found out how to rectify the error. He pressed Flamsteed to give his opinion of the theory of the instrument, but apparently without success. Molyneux professed himself pleased with the instrument: 'I can take the time of day or night thereby to five seconds without any calculation of triangles'.[35] He wrote a book on the subject with the title *Sciothericum telescopicum: or, a new contrivance of adapting a telescope to an horizontal dial for observing the moment of time by day or night: useful in all astronomical observations and for regulating and adjusting curious pendulum watches and other time-keepers, with proper tables requisite thereto.* The book contained a detailed description of the structure and working of the instrument, with elaborate illustrations. It was printed in Dublin in 1686 and distributed by Molyneux's bookseller, W. Norman. The dedication was to Lord Clarendon (who had arrived as lord lieutenant at the beginning of that year), in appreciation of the encouragement he had given to the Dublin Philosophical Society. There were also reflections on the practical uses of natural philosophy as studied by similar societies in several parts of Europe, contrasted with the formal philosophy taught in the universities.

Clarendon's appointment was a great relief to Molyneux and his fellow protestants, who had been very apprehensive about their fate under the catholic James II. Molyneux wrote to his brother that Clarendon on his arrival had made 'a most pleasing speech, and with a more than ordinary elevated voice' declared that his majesty had heard of fears that the act of settlement (guaranteeing land titles) was to be altered, but 'gave them his princely word that he never had such a thought; neither would he disturb any man in the least in his possession or religion'.[36] Clarendon was the king's brother-in-law and a strong anglican. On personal grounds also he was congenial to Molyneux, as he was a cultivated man, with a fine library, and a fellow of the Royal Society. Molyneux presented him with the *Sciothericum* instrument. Clarendon sent a copy of the book to John Evelyn with a suggestion that Evelyn should encourage Molyneux to undertake a natural history of Ireland.[37]

Molyneux demonstrated the use of the instrument to the Dublin Philosophical Society, claiming that it had 'improved the art of dialling, before lame and imperfect, to that accurateness that he can determine the time of day to two seconds, and by a most ingenious application of telescopic sights to it has made it so universal that by any known star he can determine most exactly the time also of the night'.[38] He sent his brother a copy of the book to present on his behalf to the Royal Society, and a summary, without comment, was published in the *Philosophical Transactions*.[39] Summaries also appeared in the *Acta Eruditorum* of Leipzig and in Le Clerc's *Bibliothèque universelle*. Le Clerc remarked that he had not seen the actual book but had been sent the title and a summary in English, which he had translated: he requested 'those who wish to send us such things to make them a little more extended and not to be content only to indicate the substance but to explain briefly some of the principles'.[40] Molyneux professed himself well pleased with the reception given to the instrument, 'a contrivance which, I may say without vanity, has not displeased at home and has been well received abroad'.[41] But it seems never to have been popular, though as late as 1703 one was ordered by Trinity College, Cambridge.[42] One of his biographers remarked: 'It is certain he was not a little fond of the invention . . . however it must be confessed that our author's instrument never came into general use'.[43]

Soon after returning to Dublin in the autumn of 1685 Molyneux suggested to Sir Richard Bulkeley, who was a fellow of both the Dublin Society and the Royal Society, that Ashe and himself might be admitted to the Royal Society. Both were proposed and elected shortly afterwards, though there was considerable delay in informing them of the election.[44] Molyneux was a genuine, but not uncritical, admirer of the Royal Society. He regretted the divisions that had shown themselves there. He was sorry that Francis Aston, with whom he had become very friendly, had given up the secretaryship: 'I fear these animosities will do the society no service'. He was apprehensive that some members 'would fain model the rest to their useless way of philosophising, I mean in search of shells, insects etc . . . and will condemn mathematics as a hindrance in investigating nature'.[45] The comment comes as something of a surprise, considering the great variety of subjects on which Molyneux was prepared to speak and write. He represented the earlier spirit of the Royal Society in which there were as yet no signs of fission between the mathematicians and the collectors of natural curiosities, the professionals and the amateurs. Halley later explained to Molyneux that he supposed that Aston had struck for a higher salary and had done so in such a manner as to lose several friends. The society had therefore decided to have honorary secretaries in future and a salaried clerk assistant, and appointed Halley to the latter post. Molyneux was concerned for the administration of the society and the regular publication of the *Philosophical Transactions*. He hoped that Halley's appointment would remedy matters: 'but I fear he may love his ease a little too much'. Halley frankly admitted to

Molyneux 'that torpid malady whereby I have so well deserved to lose many of my friends'.[46] However, relations between the two men became very friendly.

Molyneux had returned to Dublin to find that his son, born in the preceding April, had developed into a fine child. But his hopes were dashed in February 1686, when the child suddenly fell ill and died in a few moments. He himself became ill and was troubled with fever and ague all that spring. His wife gave birth to a second child in April 1687, a daughter who died within two days.

After William had left Paris, Thomas remained there for some time, visiting hospitals and becoming acquainted with French savants. He intended to go on to the famous medical school at Montpellier and then on to Italy. But his father foresaw that trouble was likely to arise in King James's dominions and that it might be difficult to keep Thomas supplied with money. So he persuaded him to cut his travels short. Thomas arrived in London in March 1686, but he was reluctant to return to Dublin till he was qualified for his M.D., five years after his bachelor's degree. In London he renewed his acquaintance with members of the Royal Society, was proposed for membership in June and elected in November.[47] He also visited Oxford and renewed his acquaintance with Dr Plot, who entrusted him with copies of his *Natural history of Staffordshire* for presentation to William and others in Ireland.[48] Thomas returned to Dublin in April 1687.

The anxieties of protestants in Ireland had multiplied after the abrupt recall of Clarendon and the arrival of Richard Talbot, earl of Tyrconnell, as viceroy in the beginning of 1687. Tyrconnell was an enthusiastic catholic who had already transformed the army in Ireland by a systematic substitution of catholic officers and men for protestants, who were cashiered in great numbers. One of the few protestants left in high command was the Molyneuxs' friend, Lord Mountjoy, who remained master general of the ordnance. Tyrconnell was determined to complete his work by giving catholics pre-eminence in church and state. One of the victims was Molyneux's father-in-law, Sir William Domville, who was turned out of the office of attorney general. Molyneux himself lost his position as joint surveyor general. There was a strong impression that Tyrconnell's purge was to be accompanied by a revision of the restoration land settlement, on which the titles of most protestants in Ireland, including the Molyneuxs, depended. Preparations for a parliament, which it was feared would reverse the land settlement, included the withdrawal of the charters of the town corporations, which had been protestant monopolies. The new charters provided for catholic majorities, which would have the right to elect most of the members of a new parliament. Catholics were jubilant, there was much unrest in the countryside, and rents were difficult to collect. For the time being this was less of a problem on the Molyneuxs' estate of Castle Dillon in County Armagh, where the tenants were protestant, but in Limerick and Kildare, where they also had estates, conditions were rapidly deteriorating. Not surprisingly, Molyneux's letters to Flamsteed became irregular, but he was sure that Flamsteed would understand why. In May 1687 he wrote to Flamsteed: 'You know our present condition here too well to expect from us any vigorous advancement of philosophy or mathematics; these like poetry, *secessum et otia quaerunt* [need retreat and leisure]'. Flamsteed sent him a list of satellite eclipses for the coming year with the remark: 'I know you are not in very encouraging circumstances, yet you will be desirous to have them . . . I hope when they become observable in the evenings you will take care to get some of them observed.'[49] Molyneux was preoccupied with personal and public anxieties and we have only one letter from him to Flamsteed for 1688.

Affairs in Ireland became still more critical with the events of that year: the birth of a son to James, the landing of William of Orange, the flight of James. There was a state of anarchy over much of the Irish countryside, and protestants were panic-stricken by rumours of an intended massacre. Tyrconnell continued at the head of the government in James's name, and a mass emigration of protestants began. William Molyneux and his family remained for some time in Dublin, but at the end of January 1689 they decided to leave. Thomas went with them, but their parents stayed behind. Samuel said it was hardly worth crossing the sea to preserve the little residue of his life, but he advised the younger generation to seek safety. William's father-in-law was also determined to stay, and the parting was a sad affair for what had been a most united family. After a difficult crossing they landed at Liverpool and then made for Chester, where many of the protestant refugees had settled. The Molyneux family rented a house outside the north gate, where they remained for nearly two years. They were not in the same distress as many of the refugees, as William had provided himself with money and Thomas was able to contribute from his medical practice. But it was an anxious time for them. They were cut off from communication with their parents and were uncertain whether they would ever see Ireland again. In March 1689 William paid a visit to London where he was able to see Flamsteed and attend a meeting of the Royal Society—for the first time since his election. In the course of the meeting he gave the society an account of a clock he had seen in Coventry which showed the motions of the sun and moon sufficiently accurately to enable eclipses to be predicted. It also showed the planetary systems. He was asked to make a further inspection on his return journey to Chester and give the society an exact description.[50] His wife gave birth to another son, born in Chester on 18 July 1689. The child was called Samuel for his grandfather, and lived to be a source of great interest and pride to his father.

During the summer of 1689 the hopes of the Chester exiles were raised by the Williamite expeditionary force that was gathering in the neighbourhood of the town under the command of the veteran duke of Schomberg. However, though this force gained some initial success in the north of Ireland it failed to overthrow the Jacobite regime, and the exiles had to endure a winter of depression. Molyneux wrote to Flamsteed in September 1689 that he was 'tossed about, sometimes with faint hopes, but generally with distracting fears, labouring under the public, and not only my own private, calamity'.[51] Hopes rose again when King William prepared to fight in Ireland himself, and on 8 June 1690 reached Chester, where his men and the ships to carry them were waiting. This time the news was better: William defeated his rival on 1 July 1690 (O.S.) at the battle of the Boyne. James fled to France and William entered Dublin in triumph. Fighting was to go on for more than a year after that, but the immediate reaction of the protestants of Ireland was that the worst was over and that they could confidently expect the restoration of their own ascendancy.

William and Thomas at once returned to Dublin to see their parents, who were overjoyed at the reunion. William's father-in-law, Sir William Domville, had died the previous year. William stayed in Dublin for a fortnight and then returned to Chester to fetch his family. On the way he was arrested in Wales by soldiers who confused him with a member of the Jacobite family of Molyneuxs, and he had some difficulty in establishing his Williamite credentials. When he reached Chester he found that his wife was sickly and unfit to travel; so they remained there for some months longer. Meanwhile he was selected by the Williamite government in Dublin to become a commissioner for stating the accounts of the army. The post entailed a considerable amount of work as the pay of the large army that William employed in Ireland had fallen into heavy arrears. The accounts had to be sorted out between the English and Irish exchequers, and both parliaments pressed for statements. The English commons blamed the Irish commissioners for delay. The salary of £500 *per annum* was hardly earned.[52]

Molyneux returned to Dublin in December, leaving his wife and child to follow in January 1691. Soon after they had reached Dublin the boy fell sick and there were fears for his life. Happily he recovered, but the strain was too much for his mother, who fell ill again: 'she was seized with a shortness of breath, accompanied by a violent cough, and then grew dropsical'.[53] She died on 9 May 1691. To add to Molyneux's worries his old father handed over to him the management of the Castle Dillon estate in County Armagh.[54] This required considerable attention as the area had been in the war zone; the protestant tenants had been driven out during the Jacobite regime, and new leases had to be negotiated. Molyneux found it hard to find time and spirit for the important work on optics that had been his preoccupation for so many years and was now ripe for publication.

V

DIOPTRICS

LIGHT and its properties were a major field of scientific study ever since Galileo's 'optic glass' transformed astronomy. Descartes's *Dioptrique* set out the laws of refraction, but his interpretation was to be modified and the subject studied in depth by younger men. However, neither Newton's *Optics* nor Huygens's *Dioptrica* had been published when Molyneux was grappling with the problems of dioptrics—the principles of refraction through transparent media such as lenses.[1] Molyneux was strongly attracted to the subject: he confessed himself 'much enamoured with optics, for in them there is such a mixture of physics and mathematics that renders this study very pleasing'.[2] But his wife's blindness may have given him a special interest in the subject. In this, as in other scientific fields, he was greatly helped in his difficulties by both Flamsteed and Halley. Their support made him feel less isolated in Dublin, where there was no authority to whom he could turn for advice or help.

In his correspondence with Flamsteed the first indication of Molyneux's interest in the theory of optics was an expression of dissatisfaction with the thirty-fourth proposition in Kepler's *Dioptrice*, that the angle of refraction was directly proportional to the angle of incidence.[3] He also mentioned an Oxford pamphlet, with the title *Propositions concerning optic glasses*.[4] From then on the correspondence often touches on optical problems. Molyneux posed them and was tireless in his determination to gain a thorough understanding of each point. Flamsteed was an exemplary instructor, patient and ready to explain at great length. He was an encouraging teacher, who assured Molyneux of his progress in grasping the essentials of optics. Both men were agreed that previous writers had not treated the subject satisfactorily. Flamsteed maintained that he had learned most from 'some loose papers of Mr Gascoigne, an ingenious young gentleman who was slain at York fight . . . and all that I know of glasses is but a superstructure on that foundation'.[5] Gascoigne was a self-taught mathematician who invented the micrometer and was the first to combine telescopic sights with a quadrant. After his death at Marston Moor in 1644 his papers were preserved by a scientific-minded neighbour who allowed Flamsteed to examine them.

Molyneux's first discourse to the embryo Dublin Society, on 5 October 1683, was on an optical subject, the illusion that the moon (or any heavenly body) is larger when it is on the horizon than when high in the sky, a problem that had first been discussed in the second century A.D. by Ptolemy. Molyneux outlined the views of Descartes, Hobbes and Gassendi on this phenomenon and pronounced them to be unsatisfactory and erroneous.[6] He seems to have thought over the problem for the next few years before writing a long letter to Halley on the subject.[7] He told Flamsteed that Halley had asked him for the paper: 'but since I sent it to him I have wished I had sent it first to be examined by you. But I know you may have it from him if you will take that trouble.'[8] In view of Flamsteed's feelings about Halley this was less than tactful, and Flamsteed made no comment. Halley, as clerk to the Royal Society, asked Dr John Wallis, Savilian professor of geometry at Oxford, to give his opinion on Molyneux's letter. The letter and Wallis's comments were then published in the *Philosophical Transactions*.[9] Descartes had attributed the illusion to the fact that the moon on the horizon was compared with terrestrial objects, while no such comparison could be made with the moon when high in the sky. To this Molyneux answered that this was 'much below the accustomed accuracy of the noble Descartes': if his argument was correct Molyneux could increase the apparent size of the meridional moon simply by viewing it against a cluster of chimneys or the ridge of a hill, which would give a basis for comparison. Besides the horizontal moon rising over a smooth sea appeared no less enlarged than when seen against objects on land. Hobbes had drawn an elaborate figure to show that equal angles subtended from the eye would cover a larger arc of sky on the horizon than in the meridian. Molyneux admitted that Hobbes's geometry was demonstrable, but he maintained that the diagram was artificial: Hobbes was arguing 'as confidently as if nature would accommodate herself to his scheme, and he not obliged to accommodate his scheme to nature'. Gassendi had written 'four large epistles' on the subject, arguing that the moon near the horizon was looked at through foggy air and shed a feebler light, so that the pupil of the viewer's eye was expanded and the image thrown on the retina enlarged. Molyneux pointed out that enlarging the pupil did not increase the projection on the retina, although several writers on optics maintained that it did. Wallis's explanation was that the number of intermediate objects between the eye and the horizon suggested that the moon in that position was further away than when seen alone in the meridional sky.

The phenomenon is philosophically of importance and was

examined at length by George Berkeley in his *Essay towards a new theory of vision*.[10] He agreed with Molyneux's criticism of Descartes and other writers, and he had no high opinion of Wallis's explanation. Berkeley's own view was that the atmosphere caused greater interference with the rays from the horizontal than from the meridional moon. The moon on the horizon appeared fainter and therefore further away than in the meridional position, with the result that the viewer assumed it to be larger. The problem has continued to arouse interest in our own day, and from time to time one or other of the older theories has been advanced as the true explanation of the phenomenon.[11]

At another meeting of the embryo society, on 10 December 1683, Molyneux read a paper on the problem of double vision. He wished to confute the prevailing view, supported by such writers as Gassendi and Tacquet, that only one eye was used to look at an object: if both eyes were used, it was argued, the object would appear in two places at the same time. He drew a distinction between looking, in which the two eyes focused on a particular object, and seeing, in which an object could appear double, with a second image distinct from that on which the eyes focused. If the right eye closed the image on the right disappeared, if the left eye closed the image on the left disappeared. He described experiments with candles and supported his thesis with diagrams. He sent his paper to the Royal Society, which entered it in the letter-book, though it was not published in the *Philosophical Transactions*.[12] Curiously, he does not seem even to have referred to the problem in his correspondence with Flamsteed.

Molyneux took issue with the writer of an article in the *Journal des sçavans* for 17 September 1685, who posed the question why four glasses in a telescope should show objects erect. The writer argued that, as one glass showed an erect image, two glasses an inverted, and three glasses an erect, it would be logical that four glasses should again show an inverted image. Molyneux said that this was based on a misunderstanding. A telescope consisting of an object glass and three eyeglasses should be thought of as two telescopes, each containing a pair of glasses. The object glass and the first eyeglass together inverted the image; the second eyeglass restored it to the erect position and the third eyeglass showed the image erect, as it received it. He sent his paper to the Royal Society, where it was read on 3 November 1686. It was then printed in the *Philosophical Transactions* with the title 'A dioptric problem'. He also sent a summary to Le Clerc who published a translation of it in his *Bibliothèque universelle* with the acid comment that the problem could only have been posed by someone who was not well versed in dioptrics. Flamsteed expressed his appreciation of Molyneux's paper and remarked that the Frenchman (who had written in the *Journal des sçavans*) seemed not to understand glasses.[13]

Towards the end of 1686 Flamsteed told Molyneux that he was working on a treatise about dioptrics; it would form part of a wider study and would include what Flamsteed had written to him about the effects of combining lenses in a telescope. He made it clear that his demonstrations were communicated to Molyneux for his private use, and not for publication. Molyneux expressed his pleasure that Flamsteed was going to publish and urged him not to delay, as there was a danger that Flamsteed's prolonged silence would be the subject of hostile criticism. Flamsteed might be assured that his information would be as safe with Molyneux as in his own breast.[14]

Molyneux was apparently sceptical about the prospect of Flamsteed's work being brought to the point of publication. At any rate, when he had fled from the troubles of Ireland at the beginning of 1689 and had found shelter in Chester, he sought distraction from his anxieties in assembling the material he had collected on dioptrics. He had been able to bring some of his books and papers with him, but not his instruments. He made no reference to the progress of his work in the desultory correspondence he had with Flamsteed until he had completed the draft of a book and even written the dedication to the Royal Society. The dedication, dated 17 April 1690, paid enthusiastic tribute to the 'philosophical societies of Europe (to whom your institution has shown the way and been an illustrious example)' for their work in promoting experiment and observation and throwing over the jargon invented by commentators on Aristotle. He singled out for special commendation 'the incomparable Mr Locke, who in his *Essay concerning human understanding* has rectified more received mistakes and delivered more profound truths established on experience and observation for the direction of man's mind in the prosecution of knowledge . . . than are to be met with in all the volumes of the ancients'. Molyneux added a warning against attempts to assign causes to natural phenomena: 'what is the cause of gravity is clearly unknown to us'.

An 'admonition to the reader', also dated 17 April 1690, justified *Dioptrica nova* and, in particular, claimed complete novelty for the geometrical method of calculating the path of a ray. He acknowledged as his source Flamsteed, who had derived his own information from Gascoigne's unpublished papers. He added that he had begun to write the work in Latin, but had decided to change to English,

Sciothericum Telescopicum;

O R,

A New Contrivance of Adapting a

TELESCOPE

TO AN

Horizontal Dial

FOR OBSERVING

The moment of Time by Day or Night.

Useful in all *Astronomical Observations*, and for Regulating and Adjusting

Curious *Pendulum-Watches* and other *Time-Keepers*, With proper *Tables* Requisite thereto.

By *William Molyneux* Esq; *Fellow* of the *Royal Society*, and of that in *Dublin*.

DUBLIN,

Printed by *Andrew Crook* and *Samuel Helsham*, at the *Printing-House* on *Ormond-Key*; and are to be sold by *W. Norman* in *Dame-street*, and *S. Helsham* and *El. Dobson* Booksellers in *Castle-street*, 1686.

WILL.^M MOLLINEAUX
of the City of Dublin
Efq.^r

in which nothing of the sort had so far been published: 'I am sure there are many ingenious heads, great geometers and masters in mathematics, who are not so well skilled in Latin'. If, however, there was a demand from foreigners for the book he might consider publishing a Latin version.

Early in May 1690 Molyneux disclosed, apparently for the first time, to Flamsteed what he had undertaken: 'whenever the troublesome thoughts of the misery of my poor country would permit me (which indeed was but seldom), I have diverted my mind by the consideration of dioptrics, and have put the last hand to an idle work of this kind, which I now design for the press'. He asked for permission to publish material that Flamsteed had communicated to him, assuring him that full acknowledgment would be given. He added, rather tactlessly, that in several cases he had given his own alternative solutions in addition to those provided by Flamsteed.[15]

Flamsteed might well be taken aback by the news that Molyneux, without having referred to it in previous letters, had completed a work on dioptrics in which he had included some of Flamsteed's own solutions. However, his answer was cordial. He wished the book 'an happy appearance in the world', and freely consented to Molyneux publishing anything that he had received from him. He added that he himself had not the leisure to put together the material from his lectures on dioptrics and his further thoughts on the subject. He warned Molyneux that what he had written in his letters might require checking, and gave him leave to amend any looseness of expression. Molyneux's book would save him from the importunities of 'some fools who are frequently pressing me to give those dioptric propositions and an account of the telescope and the effect of compounded glass'. He ended his letter in the warmest terms: 'I wish therefore an happy progress of your work. That God would bless you with good news from your friends in Ireland is the constant hearty prayer of, Sir, your affectionate friend and humble servant.'[16]

Flamsteed also warned Molyneux not to publish his book if he had not read Huygens's *Traité de la lumière*. This work, which Flamsteed offered to send, propounded the wave theory of light in preference to the corpuscular theory then in vogue and accepted by Newton and others. Molyneux replied thanking Flamsteed for the freedom and candour of his letter: 'and [I] do thankfully embrace the liberty you therein grant me'. He admitted that he had not heard of Huygens's book, but explained that in his own book he took no notice of the theories of Descartes and others on the physical properties of light, though he had referred to a concept of Leibniz. This was that the creator of all things had made light proceed by the shortest direct way. Flamsteed answered that if Molyneux had not touched on 'the nature of light or the reason of reflection or refraction' he might 'speed the book to the press'. In fact Molyneux did give his views on the nature of light and revealed himself as a believer in the corpuscular theory. Among the proofs that he adduced for this were refraction and the calculable speed of light, for which he cited Newton's *Principia* and the 'labours of the ingenious Mr Flamsteed and Mr Halley'.[17]

The dedication to the Royal Society is dated 17 April 1690, and it appears that the manuscript was then submitted to the society for approval. At the meeting of 4 June 1690 it was noted that Sir John Hoskins, the vice-president 'with the good liking of the society' was pleased to give his approbation to the printing of the book. This imprimatur, which satisfied the licensing law, was inserted in the printed version. In August 1690 Molyneux went to London to arrange for the publication of *Dioptrica nova*. There is no evidence that he met Flamsteed on this occasion or ever showed him the manuscript. Instead, he consulted Halley, who undertook to see the manuscript through the press; the publisher was Benjamin Tooke. Halley allowed Molyneux to include as an appendix his own important theorem for finding the focus of a spherical glass. Molyneux was delighted with it, telling Halley that it was 'so very fine I can never be able sufficiently to admire it'. It is likely that the *Dioptrica* benefited in other ways from Halley's advice. Molyneux wrote to him: 'if my book do no other good in the world I should think time well bestowed by putting so ingenious a head in these inquiries'.[18]

The title page is dated 1692 and it appears that the book was published early in the year. It was a substantial volume: 301 pages of text and a number of figures and illustrations finely drawn on pull-out pages. The first part consisted of fifty-nine propositions set out in Euclidean fashion, the proof of later propositions founded on those already established. The last two treated of microscopes and magic lanterns; the rest were concerned with the properties of telescopic lenses, but the twenty-eighth proposition dealt with the nature of sight: in Molyneux's words 'the manner of plain vision with the naked eye is expounded'. In the course of his exposition he observed that the image thrown on the retina was inverted and asked how it was that the eye saw the object erect. His answer was that, properly speaking, it was not the eye that saw erect objects; the eye was only an instrument by which the soul saw the object, and it was not within the scope of his treatise to inquire into the soul's faculty. However, he added that 'erect' and 'inverted' were only terms relative to the position of parts of an object in relation to the centre of the earth: up or down, nearer or farther. Seeing involved a judgment that the ray striking the lower part of the retina had come from the upper part of the object, and that the ray striking the upper part of the retina had come from the lower part of the object: the mind had a natural ability to 'hunt back' along each ray of light from the point of retinal stimulation to the corresponding part of the object. An analogy might be found in the case of a man standing on his head who would make a correct judgment about the position of the objects that he saw.

This was a problem that had puzzled thinkers from Leonardo da Vinci onwards and is still the subject of debate. Huygens observed that Molyneux had given a good explanation of it.[19] Berkeley examined the question at considerable length in his *Essay on a new theory of vision*. He argued that the image on the retina would be seen inverted only by another person looking at it, who would see the whole eye as well as the image on the retina. The person so looked at would have on his retina the image not only of an object but of its surroundings in relation to which the object would be erect.[20] Berkeley dismissed Molyneux's explanation as contrary to experience: 'crossing and tracing of the rays is never thought on by children, idiots, or in truth by any other, save only by those who have applied themselves to the study of optics'.[21] Berkeley attached great importance to his own interpretation of the problem: 'the solution of this knot about inverted images seems the principal part in the whole optic theory, the most difficult perhaps to comprehend, but the most deserving of our attention, and when rightly understood the surest way to lead the mind into a thorough knowledge of the true nature of vision'.[22]

The thirty-first proposition dealt with the apparent position of objects seen through convex glasses. The ninth section of this proposition took the case of an object lying beyond the focus of a convex glass and stated that, to an eye placed between the glass and the 'distinct base' (image produced by the rays from the object after passing through the glass), the apparent position of the object could not be determined. This was a problem that had baffled Isaac Barrow, Newton's predecessor at Cambridge, and students of philosophy have named it the Barrovian case. How far away would an object appear to be that was seen by converging rays, as the eye was between the glass and the point where the rays met at the image? Barrow reasoned that the less diverging were the rays the further off the object appeared to be. If the rays were very divergent it would appear close, if they were parallel it would appear very remote. Should it not therefore appear to be even further remote if the rays were converging? But this did not tally with experience: as the eye was placed further back from the glass and moved towards the position of the image the object appeared to come nearer until it disappeared in mere confusion. Barrow admitted that this seemed inconsistent with the principles of optics. He was not prepared to abandon those principles and argued that in this case 'something peculiar lies hid, which being involved in the subtlety of nature will perhaps hardly be discovered till such time as the manner of vision is more perfectly made known'. The 'candid' Barrow left the difficulty to be solved by others, and Molyneux declared that he would follow his example. But he could not resist offering a tentative solution, that the apparent position of the object would be as far in front of the eye as the image was behind the eye. Huygens, who approved generally of Molyneux's book noted on this passage: 'he makes much inquiry about the place of the image and says he sticks in the same way as Barrow: this, of course, because he wants the distance to be judged with one eye'. Berkeley had reservations about the geometrical approach to optics: lines and angles had no real existence in nature, being only a hypothesis formed by mathematicians that they might treat of optics in a geometrical way. He devoted considerable space to the Barrovian case which, he thought, even if there were no other objections to the theories of writers on optics would be enough to bring their credit in question. He disagreed with the solution offered by Molyneux which, if the object were one-and-a-half focal lengths from the glass would, on the standard formula, put its apparent position twice as far away as its real position: a result that, Berkeley said, 'manifestly contradicts experience, the object never appearing at furthest beyond its due distance'. Berkeley's position was that it was not angles that enabled an observer to judge distance, but the greater or less confusedness with which the object was perceived. Whether the rays diverged or converged the image became more confused as the divergency or convergency increased and the nearer the object appeared to be.[23]

In the sixteenth, seventeenth, and eighteenth propositions, in addition to Molyneux's own solutions, those of Flamsteed were given, with acknowledgment to 'my esteemed friend, the learned and ingenious Mr John Flamsteed, Reg. Astr.'. This first part was very much of a textbook. Its aims were limited and the philosophical atmosphere of Newton's later work on the subject was altogether absent. But the treatment was thorough and must have involved considerable effort and sustained application.

The second part of the book consisted of a series of chapters on 'several dioptric miscellanies', among them refraction and light, glasses for defective eyes, and telescopic instruments. It was written in a more popular style and at places, as in the account of the planets, bordered on the fanciful. This part of the book was dedicated to his friend Henry Osborne of Dardistown, County Meath, and acknowledged the help he had received from Osborne on dioptric problems. This second part also included Molyneux's demonstration that four convex glasses in a telescope showed objects erect (already published in the *Philosophical Transactions* of the Royal Society), and 'an optic problem of double vision', a revised version of the paper he had read to the Dublin Philosophical Society in 1683. He called in tennis to illustrate his point that we habitually see with both eyes together: 'the best player in the world hoodwinking one eye shall be beaten by the greatest bungler that ever handled a racquet, unless he be used to the trick and then by custom he gets a habit of using one eye only'.[24]

According to Molyneux, Flamsteed, to whom a copy of the book was presented, took offence because his solutions of certain propositions were given as alternatives to Molyneux's solutions and placed after them. It seems more probable that Flamsteed was hurt that he had not been shown the manuscript before publication, and that, after all the help he had given Molyneux with dioptric problems, he had been ignored and Halley entrusted with the publication. There is no record of the letter in which Flamsteed conveyed his sentiments. He seems to have spoken disparagingly of the book, observing that it contained several mistakes that were not mere printer's errors. Molyneux made several attempts to secure a reconciliation, but met with no success. The breach was final and Molyneux abandoned the effort to mend it: 'at last I slighted the friendship of a man of so much ill nature and irreligion, how ingenious and learned soever'.[25]

It is understandable that Molyneux, who had returned to Ireland at the end of 1690, should have relied on Halley to see the book through the press. Halley was the younger man, Molyneux's contemporary, and he was accustomed in his work for the Royal Society to dealing with printers and publishers. Flamsteed was ten years older and temperamentally critical. He would undoubtedly have subjected Molyneux to cross-examination on the details of his work, and in Molyneux's circumstances that would have been an ordeal difficult to face. All the same, one is left with the impression that Flamsteed was shabbily treated after the enormous pains he had taken to instruct Molyneux in the niceties of dioptrics.

It is agreeable to know that, twenty years later, when Molyneux's son Samuel visited Flamsteed at Greenwich he was received with the greatest kindness on account of the friendship there had once been between Flamsteed and his father. Flamsteed evidently responded to the young man's interest in astronomy. He showed him his instruments and allowed him to take the sun's meridian height by his mural quadrant. He also showed him a number of his writings on astronomical problems and invited him to come to the observatory any night he pleased. Samuel's subsequent achievements as an astronomer may owe something to his cordial reception by Flamsteed, who seems to have mellowed in old age and certainly showed a commendable readiness not to allow his former bitterness towards the father to affect his treatment of the son.[26]

Molyneux took care to bring the book to the notice of the intelligentsia. Tooke was asked to distribute a number of copies— to Oxford, Cambridge, the Royal Society; to Newton, Halley and Flamsteed. Molyneux inscribed the copy he presented to Trinity College, Dublin, as the humble offering of a most grateful alumnus. His old tutor, Dr Palliser, and Provost Ashe also received copies. Hooke, Wallis and Boyle were among others in a long list of recipients noted by Molyneux in a copy of *Dioptrica* now in the British Library.[27] In spite of this, *Dioptrica nova* does not appear to have created any great sensation in the learned world. There is no reference to it in the *Philosophical Transactions,* which appeared very irregularly at this time. There was only one number in 1692— in October—and it contained no notices of books. Nor was the book noticed in continental journals, with the exception of the *Acta Eruditorum* of Leipzig.[28] That had a short notice in which Molyneux was referred to as *auctor eruditissimus* and attention was drawn to the trigonometrical basis of the book as derived from Gascoigne *via* Flamsteed. It was also pointed out that Newton's work on refraction had been followed and that Halley's theorem was set out in an appendix.

In February 1692 Huygens noted that he had been told of a treatise on dioptrics by a member of the Royal Society. He wondered if Locke was the writer. In April of that year he was sent a copy of Molyneux's book by a young German who had just come from England. He wrote to his friend, Fatio de Duillier, that he found Molyneux's description of the working of telescopes better than anything of the sort that had been done before. The young German had offered to send a Latin version of the book to a Rotterdam bookseller in the hope that he would print it, and Huygens approved of the proposal.[29] In the event a Latin translation was published in Amsterdam, to Molyneux's dismay, as he himself had been working on a Latin version of the book. Huygens made a thorough examination of *Dioptrica nova* and commented on a number of passages. He particularly praised the dedication for its condemnation of scholastic philosophy and its endorsement of the new experimental methods. On the first chapter of the second part, dealing with refraction and light, he noted that Molyneux had adopted the corpuscular theory of light: 'he should rather have said it was motion affecting the choroid of a body'. He remarked that Molyneux did not seem to have seen his book on light (*Traité de la lumière*). Huygens claimed that in that book he had given a better demonstration of the laws of reflection and refraction than had been given by Leibniz's principle, which Molyneux followed, that light took the easiest way from one point to another. He also noted that Molyneux in his treatment of the micrometer had not mentioned Huygens's fundamental treatment of it in *Systema Saturnium*. He criticised the frivolity of Molyneux's references to the strength of Mars and the beauty of Venus. His criticisms are comparatively minor, and the extent of his commentary shows that he thought the book worth close examination. Leibniz, pleased with the reference to his principle that it was the nature of light to take the shortest path, referred to *Dioptrica nova* as a very excellent book.[30]

Molyneux claimed that he had received letters approving his book from 'some of the greatest men of the age'. Huygens may have been one of the letter writers. At any rate Molyneux sent him a copy of the book. A German mathematician who expressed his admiration was Johann Christoph Sturm who wrote to Ashe to say how delighted he was to read the extracts from *Dioptrica* in the *Acta Eruditorum*. From these samples of excellent writing he could as it were 'judge the lion from a claw'.[31] Molyneux's modest aim, as he told his brother, had been to remedy the imperfections and obscurities of previous books on dioptrics and to make 'that useful part of mathematics more complete and plain'.[32] While the work was with the printer in London he set about translating it into Latin, which would enable it to reach an international readership. In the process he said he found reason to make a number of alterations. The Latin version, which he had hoped to publish, does not seem to have survived, but his copy of the English version, now in the British Library, contains a number of manuscript annotations. These included a number of addenda, but no retractions. A long list of items was headed 'new in my *Dioptrica*'. He claimed that 'of 59 propositions, whereof the first part consists, there are as good as 35 wholly new, and amongst the rest many new remarks and operations, and amongst those that are the most common their demonstrations, which in the original authors are very intricate and obscure, are here laid down in a clear and easy method. Also in the second part of seven chapters there are four wholly new and many new things and large remarks in the rest'.

Some of the publisher's stock remained unsold for several years. Benjamin Tooke the elder had handed the business over to his son— also Benjamin—who found a few complete copies and nearly two hundred that needed a few sheets and the illustrations to make them complete. The younger Benjamin did not then think it worth while to complete the imperfect copies: 'the book being only for the curious and learned readers'. But a fresh demand was created by the publication in 1708 of *Some familiar letters between Mr Locke and several of his friends,* which drew attention to Molyneux as one of Locke's chief correspondents. The fresh demand for the book thus created coincided with an increased interest in mathematics at Oxford and Cambridge. Tooke therefore decided to bring out a second edition, incorporating any changes that Molyneux's son, Samuel, might ask him to make. The second edition appeared in 1709, but it was only the original edition with a fresh title page, and no changes had been made.[33]

Dioptrica nova received favourable comment in eighteenth-century accounts of Molyneux. An English version of Bayle's *Dictionary* noted that it 'met with the best reception and has been allowed by all judges to put the subject in the clearest light'.[34] The article on Molyneux in the *Biographia Britannica* commented: 'the reader must not expect any of the more curious speculations therein, that being foreign to [the author's] design. But several of the most generally useful propositions for practice are demonstrated in a clear and easy manner, for which reason it was for many years much used by artificers, and the second part is very entertaining, especially for the history he gives of the several optical instruments and the discoveries made by them . . .'.[35] Berkeley was familiar with the book, and it has been said that his *Theory of vision* was much indebted to it on its technical side. He made a number of comments on particular points in *Dioptrica nova,* and on occasion disagreed with it.[36]

LOCKE'S FRIEND

WHEN John Locke came up to London from his country retreat at Oates in the summer of 1692 he was told by Churchill, his publisher, that a book for him had been sent by Benjamin Tooke, another London bookseller. This was *Dioptrica nova*, by William Molyneux of Dublin, which had been published by Tooke earlier in the year. There was no inscription and Locke at first thought there might be some mistake, although the very flattering reference to the *Essay concerning human understanding* in the dedication made him suspect that the author of the *Dioptrica* was the source of the gift. Churchill was assured by Tooke that this was indeed the case. Locke wrote to Molyneux to thank him for what he had said about the *Essay:* 'if my trifle could possibly be an occasion of vanity to me you have done most to make it so, since I could scarce forbear to applaud myself upon such a testimony from one who so well understands demonstration'. He added: 'you have made great advances of friendship towards me and you see they are not lost upon me'.[1]

This was the beginning of a correspondence which lasted for six years and was ended only by Molyneux's death. Most of the letters were published after Locke's death as the opening section of *Some familiar letters between Mr Locke and several of his friends* (1708). Churchill wrote to Samuel Molyneux, William's son, to say that he proposed to include Locke's correspondence with Molyneux in a forthcoming publication. Samuel sent him twenty-nine letters that Locke had written to his father, and these were combined with thirty-four from Molyneux to Locke, presumably supplied by Locke's heir, Peter King. The correspondence is marked by great friendliness on both sides, and also by a lively interchange of ideas on a number of themes that were of active concern to both writers. Molyneux clearly felt honoured by the privilege of corresponding with a distinguished philosopher whose work he greatly admired. At the same time he was not overawed and had no hesitation in offering criticisms and constructive suggestions. Locke treated Molyneux's comments with respect and made use of many of them, particularly in later editions of the *Essay*. Some of Molyneux's actions, such as his enthusiastic reception of John Toland as Locke's friend, and the introduction of references to *Two treatises of government* in the *Case of Ireland,* must have seriously disturbed Locke, but there is no sign of this in their correspondence. The letters were included in successive editions of Locke's *Collected works* and helped to give Molyneux international recognition as Locke's friend.

Molyneux's answer referred to the great respect he had for the author of the *Essay:* 'I have not in my life read any book with more satisfaction than your *Essay,* in so much that a repeated perusal of it is still more pleasant to me'. He would reckon himself happy in Locke's friendship.

Molyneux was on more delicate ground in referring to the authorship of the *Two treatises of government* and the *Letter concerning toleration:* 'neither of them carries your name and I will not venture to ask whether they are yours or not; this only I think, no name need be ashamed of either'.[2] Locke, who was particularly concerned to preserve the anonymity of the *Two treatises,* made no reference to Molyneux's hints. But he was evidently impressed by Molyneux's enthusiasm for, and study of, the *Essay.* This and the memory of his previous association with Thomas Molyneux may account for the warmth of his next letter: 'you must therefore expect to have me live with you hereafter with all the liberty and assurance of a settled friendship. For meeting with but few men in the world whose acquaintance I find much reason to covet I make more than ordinary haste into the familiarity of a rational inquirer after, and lover of, truth whenever I can light on any such.' Molyneux's mathematical bent commended him to Locke as a critic whose opinions would deserve attention: 'I find none so fit nor so fair judges as those whose minds the study of mathematics has opened'.

He invited Molyneux's help in the preparation of a second edition of the *Essay* and asked him whether it should not be considerably pared down by omitting what 'cannot but appear superfluous to an intelligent and attentive reader'.[3] This idea was quite unacceptable to Molyneux; such prolixity was completely to his taste. Locke also ːked for suggestions for filling gaps in the argument. Molyneux, who had been elected a member of parliament for Dublin University and was occupied with the session that had just begun, was able to send only a few rough notes. But he said that he had asked for the observations of 'a most learned and ingenious man', which he promised to send to Locke. This person was Ashe, now provost of Trinity College, Dublin, who was so pleased with the *Essay* that he ordered it to be read by the bachelors in the college 'and strictly examines them in their progress therein'. In his eagerness to promote Lockian studies in the university Molyneux suggested that Locke should extract from the *Essay* a textbook of logic and metaphysics, a suggestion that Locke turned down.[4]

The parliamentary session proved to be unexpectedly short, and Molyneux was able to find time for a detailed commentary on the *Essay*, which he sent to Locke at the end of 1692.[5] This and subsequent comments led to a series of amendments that Locke made in the second edition of the *Essay*, published in the spring of 1694. The exchange of views was delayed by attacks of illness which afflicted both men. Locke was very ill in the winter of 1692. This caused concern to Thomas Molyneux, who recommended the treatment prescribed for fevers by Dr Morton. Locke was dubious about Morton, an old-fashioned Galenist; he preferred to rely on the methods of Dr Sydenham. William Molyneux was confined to bed for almost five weeks in the early part of 1693 with severe colic, which left him very weak.[6]

Some of Molyneux's criticisms were designed to clear up ambiguities or points that might be misunderstood by an unwary reader. A passage (bk IV, ch. iii, sec. 6) that attributed to God the power of enabling matter to think had been 'stumbled at by some as not consistent' with a passage (ibid., sec. 10) in which the 'immateriality of God is evinced from the absolute impossibility of matters thinking'. That was not quite what Locke had said, but he accepted the criticism and expanded the former passage to make it clear to 'less attentive readers' that, though God was able to give some degree of perception to matter, yet matter could not be 'the first eternal thinking being'. He reinforced the argument by an expansion of the second passage.[7] Molyneux also proposed a clarification of two other passages which unwary readers might consider inconsistent. In one (bk II, ch. xxiii, secs 33-6) our idea of God was said to be made up of ideas we obtained from our senses. The second (bk IV, ch. xvii, sec. 2) stated that our 'knowledge of the existence of all things without us (except only of God) [was to] be had only by our senses'. Molyneux himself found no contradiction: the first passage dealt with the complex idea we had of God, the second with God's existence. Locke agreed and thought that his meaning could be mistaken only 'by a very unwary reader who cannot distinguish between an idea in the mind and the real existence of something out of the mind answering that idea'. However, he thanked Molyneux for his warning and undertook to clarify his meaning. In the second passage after 'except only of God' he added 'whose existence every man may certainly know and demonstrate to himself from his own existence'.[8]

Molyneux proposed that the chapter on the existence of God (bk IV, ch. x) should include a rebuttal of the view that the world had existed from eternity: 'I have known a pack of philosophical atheists that rely much on this hypothesis, and even Hobbes himself does somewhere allege . . . that the same arguments which are brought against the eternity of the world may serve as well against the eternity of the creator of the world'.[9] Locke, however, did not pursue this point. How did Molyneux come to know a 'pack of philosophical atheists'? There do not appear to have been any overt declarations of atheism published up to the end of Molyneux's life. It is possible that during his law-student days in restoration London he may have listened to the talk of uninhibited sceptics.

A substantial alteration of the *Essay* was made as a result of Molyneux's comment on the treatment of liberty and necessity (bk II, ch. xxi), in which he found that the 'thread seems so wonderfully fine spun in your book that at last the great question of liberty and necessity seems to vanish'. Molyneux was dissatisfied with the attribution of sin to want of understanding rather than to depravity of will: 'it seems harsh to say, that a man shall be damned because he understands no better than he does'. Locke admitted that his treatment of liberty was too fine spun: he had thought of leaving it out, but was persuaded by friends not to do so. He continued to consider weakness of understanding responsible for wrong decisions, but changed his mind on the question of what determined voluntary actions. He had given this role to the will, but now transferred it to desire.[10] He communicated his thoughts on the question to Molyneux and, to indicate the revision he proposed, sent him a list of headings, to which he did not in fact adhere. He wished Molyneux were nearer so that he could show him the whole text before it went to press. It was too long for a letter, and he would have to forgo the advantage of knowing Molyneux's views. Molyneux hesitated to pass an opinion on the 'short hints' that Locke had given him.[11] Locke then gave him a fuller account of his views on desire as a determinant of the will, and asked Molyneux to examine it by his own thoughts; he was anxious to have Molyneux's 'judicious and free thoughts . . . for you love truth for itself and me so well as to tell it me without disguise'. Molyneux replied that Locke's ideas were 'very just', and that he longed to see the second edition of the *Essay*.[12]

'The epistle to the reader' of the second edition attributed Locke's change of view to 'a closer inspection into the working of men's minds': he avowed himself 'concerned to quit and renounce any opinion of my own . . . when truth appears against it'. In the first edition (bk II, ch. xxi, sec. 29), in which will was made the determinant of action, Locke argued that 'good, then, the greater good, is that alone which determines the will'. In the second edition (ibid., sec. 35) he admitted that he, in common with the generality of mankind, had taken this for granted. But on further reflection he concluded that good did not determine the will unless there was also the desire for it. The development of this train of thought led to a radical revision and considerable lengthening of the chapter. Molyneux told Locke that he thought the revisions 'most judiciously made', and that the chapter as a whole was so well put together that nothing could shake it. He was particularly pleased by the section (44) that discussed why men should prefer to remain in this life in spite of the greater attractions of eternity.[13]

Locke asked Molyneux whether he had any new heads from logic or metaphysics to suggest for inclusion in the second edition of the *Essay*. Molyneux suggested that something more might be said about *aeternae veritates* and *principium individuationis,* which, in the first edition, were touched on in the treatment of intuitive knowledge (bk IV, ch. xvii, sec. 14) and of identity (bk I, ch. iv, sec. 4; bk II, ch. i, sec. 12).[14] Locke came to the conclusion that there was nothing to be gained by enlarging on eternal verities: all general truths were eternal verities. But his further thoughts on the *principium individuationis* resulted in a new chapter (bk II, ch. xxvii) in the second edition on identity and diversity. Locke sent Molyneux the draft of this chapter, 'which having writ only at your instance it is fit you should see and judge of it before it goes to the press'. Molyneux replied that he did not repent for the trouble to which he had put Locke in writing a chapter with 'such clear reasoning and profound judgment that convinces and delights at once'.[15] However, on rereading the draft he was unhappy about Locke's discussion of the penalty applicable to drunkards and sleepwalkers who committed offences of which they were unconscious. In both cases Locke justified punishment by law on the ground that the plea of unconsciousness might be counterfeit: but at the day of judgment 'it may be reasonable to think no one shall be made to answer for what he knows nothing of' (ibid., sec. 22). Molyneux was not so concerned about the earthly punishment of the sleepwalker, though if he were on a jury trying a sleepwalker for murder he would not violate a good conscience if he acquitted him. But he was unwilling to absolve the drunkard at the day of judgment: drunkenness was itself a crime and could not therefore be pleaded in extenuation of another crime. Locke replied that his object was to show that 'punishment is annexed to personality, and personality to consciousness': drunkenness was a special case when it destroyed consciousness. However, if Molyneux thought some further explanation should be given it could be included in the errata, as the printing of the second edition was too far advanced for incorporation in the text.[16] Molyneux was satisfied with this explanation, which was accordingly inserted in the errata of the second edition and in the text of later editions.

Locke proposed to add a chapter on Malebranche's 'hypothesis of seeing all things in God'. Some critics had traced Locke's ideas to Malebranche, and he wished to make it clear that he thought Malebranche's view unsound. But he had so little love of controversy that he had not fully made up his mind to add such a chapter. Molyneux was all in favour of a chapter on Malebranche's hypothesis. He looked on Malebranche's notions—'or rather Plato's'— as perfectly unintelligible. Locke's treatment of ideas and knowledge was confirmed by experience and observation: 'Plato's fancy has no foundation in nature, but is merely the product of his own brain'.[17] Locke did make a study of Malebranche's hypothesis, but did not include it in the *Essay*. It was separately published in his *Posthumous works* (1706).

The most notable of Molyneux's contributions to the *Essay* was tentatively put forward as a 'jocose problem' which he had posed to 'divers very ingenious men', none of whom could give the answer that Molyneux believed correct until they had been convinced by hearing his reasons. This was the problem of the blind man who had learned to distinguish by touch between a cube and a sphere: if he became able to see would he be able to make the distinction by sight without touching the objects? Molyneux thought he could not. This was not the first time that the problem had been brought to Locke's notice, though he seems not to have remembered the earlier occasion. When Molyneux had seen the abridgment of the *Essay* published in Le Clerc's *Bibliothèque universelle* in 1688, 'communicated by Mr Locke', he sent this problem to the editor who passed it on to Locke, who seems not to have taken particular note of it. Now, however, Locke told Molyneux that his ingenious problem deserved to be published to the world. In 1688 Molyneux had also asked whether the formerly blind man could know by sight that an object twenty or a thousand feet from him was out of his reach, but this did not appear in the later version.[18]

When the second edition of the *Essay* was published and Molyneux received his copy he was surprised and delighted to read the addition that Locke had made to the chapter on perception. Locke

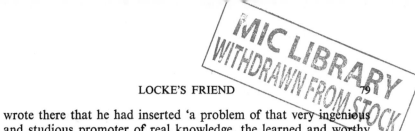

wrote there that he had inserted 'a problem of that very ingenious and studious promoter of real knowledge, the learned and worthy Mr Molyneux'. He agreed with the answer given by 'this thinking gentleman whom, though I have never had the happiness to see, I am proud to call my friend' (bk II, ch. ix, sec. 8). Molyneux was fulsome in his gratitude: 'my most honoured friend, for so you have publicly allowed me to call you, and it is a title wherein I boast more than in maces or parliament robes . . . I can only pour out my thanks to you for the favourable character under which you have transmitted me to posterity.'[19]

The problem attracted the attention of Edward Synge, an intelligent Cork clergyman who later became an archbishop. Synge, unlike Molyneux and Locke, gave an affirmative answer to the question. He distinguished between the idea that the blind man had already formed of the sphere and cube and the image that he formed when he became able to see. He thought that the similarities between the idea and the image of the sphere with its uniform shape and the cube with its divided sides would be enough to enable the man to recognise which was which without touching them. He sent his thoughts to a Dr Quayle in Dublin, who handed the letter to Molyneux. In passing it to Locke Molyneux mentioned that Synge was author of an anonymous work, *Gentleman's religion,* which was being sold as Locke's. There was 'little of mystery or enthusiastic in it, and yet the author is a clergyman; and you know that in a writer on a religious subject it is an high offence even to be silent on those abstruse points'. Locke replied that Synge's answer to Molyneux's problem showed how hard it was for 'even ingenious men to free themselves from the anticipations of sense'.[20]

Molyneux's problem had profound implications and was given different answers by philosophers, among them Leibniz and Berkeley. Rationalists answered Yes, empiricists answered No. The problem has continued to be the subject of discussion up to the present, and a substantial corpus of literature about it has accumulated.[21]

In thanking Locke for his copy of the second edition of the *Essay* Molyneux said he prized it as 'an inestimable treasure of knowledge' and expressed his complete approval of the alterations. He was particularly impressed by Locke's candid avowal that he had changed his mind about will being the determinant of action: such readiness to give up an opinion where truth required it was 'rarely to be found amongst men, and they seem to have something angelical that are so far raised above the common pitch'. Such praise was naturally most acceptable to Locke, and he returned the compliment by saying that there was no need to justify what he had said in the *Essay* about Molyneux: 'the learned world will be vouchers for me, and that in an age not very free from envy and censure'.[22] This suggests that Molyneux's standing among Locke's acquaintances was high. Molyneux gave the second edition the same careful scrutiny that he had given to the first. He sent a list of corrections which Locke promised to take care of in the next edition.[23]

Molyneux's next suggestion was that 'an elegant translation of your *Essay* into Latin would be highly acceptable to foreigners and of great use in those countries whose minds lie yet captivated in verbose, disputative philosophy'. If Locke's own supervision were not essential the translation could be done in Ireland at Molyneux's expense. Locke gladly accepted the proposal. He had not the leisure to see to the translation himself. An attempt made by a young man in Holland showed so little mastery of English or Latin that Locke had prevailed on him to abandon it. Churchill the bookseller had looked for a translator, but without success; he was willing to pay twenty pounds for a good Latin translation. Locke gave Molyneux a free hand to alter, add, or omit if he thought it desirable.[24]

The first attempt to secure a translator was a failure. Molyneux had selected a young graduate of Trinity College, Dublin, who started on the translation. Molyneux sent a specimen of the work to Locke with the hope that further experience would improve the quality. Locke did not think much of the specimen and remarked that Molyneux would have to do a good deal of correcting if the sense of the *Essay* were to be conveyed with the requisite clearness and easiness.[25] However, the young man showed so little enthusiasm for the work that Molyneux decided to look elsewhere. His choice was the Rev. Ezekiel Burridge, chancellor of the diocese of Down, who was then writing a work in Latin on the English revolution of 1688; Molyneux had seen, and admired, successive instalments of it. Before beginning his translation Burridge called on Locke, armed with a letter of introduction from Molyneux, and was pleased with his reception. Locke told Molyneux that he had at last secured a better translator than could have been expected. He had arranged for Burridge to meet Churchill and had no doubt they would reach a satisfactory agreement.[26] When Burridge returned to his diocese, he took up his task. Molyneux sent a specimen of the translation, with which Locke was not altogether satisfied. He wanted Burridge to convey the meaning in Ciceronian style without attempting to make a literal rendering of the English. He asked Molyneux not to send any more specimens: he would not have time to read them.

THE

CASE

OF

IRELAND's

Being Bound by

Acts of Parliament

I N

ENGLAND,

Stated.

B Y

William Molyneux,
of *Dublin,* Efq;

Dublin, Printed by *Joseph Ray,* and are
to be Sold at his Shop in *Skin-
ner-Row.* MDCXCVIII.

Effigies Iohannis Locke

Ex Archetypo, quod in Musæo Alexandri Geekie Chirurgi adservatur expressa.

Burridge's progress was slow, but by April 1698 Molyneux was able to tell Locke that the translation was going ahead with some speed and was of an excellent standard.[27] Molyneux did not live to see the complete work, which was published in London in 1701. A second edition, 'purged of typographical errors', was published at Leipzig in 1709.

In his first letter Molyneux had pressed Locke to publish a treatise on morals 'drawn up according to the hints you frequently give in your *Essay* of their being demonstrable according to the mathematical method'. But, though the *Essay* maintained that morality was capable of demonstration as well as mathematics, it also pointed out that moral ideas were more complex than mathematical ideas and were not susceptible of the same diagrammatic treatment. In his reply to Molyneux Locke said that he thought morality might be demonstrated, but doubted his ability to do so; however, he promised to consider the matter.[28] Molyneux reminded him of his second category of the sciences, *ars practica*, in which the chief head was ethics, 'the seeking out those rules . . . which lead to happiness, and the means to practise them'. He added that he had aroused the hopes of his friends by telling them that Locke was considering a work on ethics. However, he recognised that Locke was fully occupied with revising the *Essay*; he would not press him on ethics in the meantime.[29] But it was not long before he brought the subject up again. He asked Locke what things he had 'on the anvil', and hoped he would not forget to include his thoughts on morality. Locke promised to try, though he thought the attempt might exceed his strength. Several of his English friends had also pressed him on the subject. As soon as the second edition of the *Essay* came out, in the summer of 1694, Molyneux again asked Locke to think of a work on morality: 'this you will say is a cruelty in me, that no sooner you are rid of one trouble but I set you on another'.[30] Molyneux was supported in his demand by Burridge who considered that Locke would write an excellent book of offices or moral philosophy: 'the fine strokes which he has frequently in his esssay make me think he would perform it admirably. I wish you would try his inclinations; you may assure him I will cheerfully undertake the translation of it'. Locke answered that he had not altogether given up the idea, but he doubted whether it would be prudent in one of his age and health to undertake such a task. In any case the gospel contained such a perfect body of ethics that reason might be excused from the inquiry and leave the field to revelation.[31]

Education was a subject often referred to in the correspondence. In the spring of 1693 Molyneux told Locke that his only child was now nearly four years old, and that he was most anxious that the boy should receive the kind of education that would 'lay up a treasure of knowledge in his mind for his happiness both in this life and the next'. The family fortunes made it unnecessary for him to earn his living. Thomas Molyneux had told his brother that Locke had been writing about education when he was in Holland 'at the request of a tender father for the use of his only son'. William hoped that he would be able to apply Locke's methods in bringing up his son.[32]

Locke's thoughts on education had been substantially ready for publication by the spring of 1690, but with his usual diffidence he had postponed publication. It seems to have been Molyneux's pressure that turned the scale and induced him to go ahead. He wished, however, that Molyneux were closer at hand to give him the benefit of his opinion before he ventured to publish: 'it is so hard to find impartial freedom in one's friends or an unbiased judgment anywhere'. He was surprised that Thomas had known of the letters; he did not remember that he had spoken of them to anyone. He was not sure that he would put his name to the book and asked Molyneux to keep the secret. Molyneux replied that he was delighted that Locke's thoughts on education were to be published.[33] The book appeared anonymously in the summer of 1693, and Locke sent a copy to Molyneux, who at once set about reading it and declared that it came up to his highest expectations. His only reservation was that Locke was too severe in pronouncing that children should never be allowed to have what they craved, particularly if they cried for it. Molyneux saw no reason to deny children the same liberty of declaring their wants to their parents as the parents enjoyed of declaring their wants to God. Locke protested that he was as much in favour of innocent diversions as Molyneux was: children could ask, but must take care not to ask for anything of which their parents would not approve. Molyneux said he was satisfied with Locke's answer, but added: 'I was not the only person shocked at that passage. I find several stumble at it as taking little playthings, that children are very apt to desire and ask for, to be matters of fancy and affectation within your rule.'[34] Locke made an addition to the third edition (1695), noting that his previous observation was 'apt to be misunderstood and interpreted as if I meant that a child should never speak to his parents for anything'. But parents should distinguish between the wants of fancy and those of nature—a distinction on which he enlarged at considerable length.[35]

Locke was all for bringing children up to be hardy: clothing should not be too warm, shoes should let in the wet, washing should be in cold water. Molyneux had not applied these rules to his son 'because he is come from a tender and sickly mother': the boy was healthy, but not very strong. Locke advised gradual hardening of the boy, beginning in the spring. He quoted the example of Lady Masham's son who had been 'almost destroyed by a too tender keeping', but was now, under Locke's guidance, able to 'bear wind and weather and wet in his feet, and the cough which threatened him under that warm and cautious management has left him'.[36]

Molyneux was particularly pleased with the contrivances suggested by Locke for teaching reading and writing: a polygon of twenty-four or twenty-five sides with a letter pasted on each; sheets engraved with model writing printed in red ink to be worked over by the child with black ink. Molyneux had experimented with a similar contrivance, writing words and figures on a pack of cards with which a variety of games could be played, and at the same time the children would learn to read and count. He proposed to have his son taught shorthand, 'as useful a knack as a man of business or any scholar can be master of'. He wished he had the art himself. He strongly approved of Locke's recommendation that every gentleman's son should learn a trade. He himself had long been in favour of this, and he regretted that the 'lazy effeminate luxuriousness that overruns the nation occasions the neglect thereof'. He had intended that his son should be taught painting, but was impressed by Locke's argument to the contrary: a natural inclination would tempt the boy to spend too much time on painting to the neglect of other studies; if he had no inclination the exercise would be a waste of time; in any case recreation should not be sedentary.[37]

Almost a year later Molyneux wrote that his son was now five years old and 'of a most towardly and promising disposition, bred exactly, as far as his age permits, to the rules' prescribed by Locke. He could read very well and was now ripe for more advanced study. Could Locke find him a tutor, who would get a good handsome apartment in Molyneux's house and be expected to teach Latin to the young Samuel and a few other boys? If the tutor also knew French so much the better. He would be generously treated: 'he should eat at my own table and have his lodging, washing, firing, and candle light in my house . . . and besides this I should allow him twenty pounds per annum'. Molyneux would pay his travel charges to Ireland and, if a trial period were not satisfactory, back to England. If all went well he would hope to keep the tutor till the boy came of age. Locke made inquiries about a tutor and recommended Mr Gibbs, a candidate for the ministry of the Church of Scotland. Molyneux thanked Locke for his trouble but did not

wish to divert Gibbs from his vocation; he would try to find a
tutor in Ireland.[38] A tutor was found, and next year Molyneux wrote
to Locke: 'were it not too nigh approaching to vanity, I could tell
you of extraordinary effects your method of education has had on
my little boy'. Later that year Molyneux reported that the boy was
now six years old. When he was five, besides being able to read, he
could point out 'all the noted parts, countries, and cities of the
world' on the globes. When he was five and a half he could understand latitude and longitude, differences of time, and the antipodes:
all done by way of recreation without rebuke or punishment. 'By
the time he was six he could manage a compass, ruler, and pencil
very prettily and perform many little geometrical tricks.' He had
been three months at Latin and the tutor was 'as nigh as he can'
following Locke's method of teaching it. The boy had 'been shown
some dogs dissected and can give some little account of the grand
traces of anatomy'. His character was completely satisfactory; he
was 'obedient and observant to the nicest particular, and at the same
time sprightly, playful, and active'.[39] It is a relief to know that this
intensive upbringing had no ill effects on Samuel in later life.

In 1697 Locke told Molyneux that Pierre Coste, the Huguenot
who had translated *Thoughts concerning education* and *The reasonableness of Christianity* into French and was engaged on the translation of the *Essay,* was anxious to obtain a post as tutor in a
private house; he could read English but could not speak it.
Molyneux replied that he would have been very happy to have
Coste, but he was committed to his present tutor under whom the
boy was making good progress. However, he was trying to find a
position for the tutor and so asked for some further particulars of
Coste. Some months later Locke told Molyneux that Coste was
now at Oates, employed as tutor to Lady Masham's son.[40]

When the third edition of *Thoughts concerning education* appeared
in the summer of 1695 Locke asked Churchill to send a copy to
Molyneux, whose opinion he was anxious to obtain on the changes
he had made: 'I expect your opinion of the additions, which have
much increased the bulk of the book. And, though I think all that I
have said right, yet you are the man I depend on for a fair and free
censure, not inclined either to flatter or to quarrel. You know not
of what value a knowing man that is a sincere lover of truth is, nor
how hard to be found.' Molyneux expressed his approval of the
changes in a manner satisfactory to Locke, who replied: 'you are
a father, and are concerned not to be deceived, and therefore I
expect you will not flatter me in this point'.[41]

In the summer of 1695 Locke published, anonymously, a tract

entitled *The reasonableness of Christianity, as delivered in the scriptures.* This was a statement of the basic elements of Christianity, the beliefs required to constitute a Christian. Apart from the belief in God as creator and orderer of the world the main part of the tract was an exposition, supported by much quotation from scripture, that Jesus was the Messiah promised by God. Other doctrines, such as the Trinity, original sin, everlasting punishment, were not included in the essentials. The tract drew a quick rejoinder from a Cambridge divine named Edwards who attacked it as Socinian and hinted strongly that Locke was the author. Locke replied, again anonymously, with a vindication, to which Edwards riposted with *Socinianism unmask'd.* Locke did not refer to the controversy in his correspondence with Molyneux; it was to Philip Limborch, the Dutch theologian, that he acknowledged in confidence his authorship of the tract. But Molyneux evidently read the tract and the subsequent exchanges. In June 1696 he wrote to Locke: 'I find by some little pieces I have lately met with that you are the reputed author of the *Reasonableness of Christianity*; whether it be really so or not I will not presume to inquire, because there is no name to the book; this only I will venture to say on that head that whoever is the author or vindicator thereof, he has gotten as weak an adversary in Mr Edwards to deal with as a man could wish; so much unmannerly passion and Billingsgate language I have not seen any man use'. Locke answered: 'what you say of the *Reasonableness of Christianity* gives me occasion to ask your thoughts of that treatise and also how it passes amongst you there, for here, at its first coming out, it was received with no indifferency, some speaking of it with great commendation, but most censuring it as a very bad book'. Molyneux told Locke that the book was approved of by 'candid unprejudiced men that dare speak their thoughts'. He had asked a 'very learned and ingenious prelate' how he liked it: 'he told me, very well, and that if my friend Mr Locke writ it 'twas the best book he ever laboured at; but, says he, if I should be known to think so I should have my lawns torn from my shoulders'.[42] It seems likely that the prelate was Ashe, who had become bishop of Cloyne in 1695. His reaction suggests that he was more tolerant of unorthodoxy than were some of his fellow-bishops. Molyneux's religious attitude was similar to Locke's, a belief in an all-wise providence, with the minimum of doctrinal accompaniments.

Locke's religious views were attacked in 1697 by a more formidable opponent, Edward Stillingfleet, bishop of Worcester, who had long enjoyed a reputation as a controversialist. Stillingfleet's *Discourse in vindication of the doctrine of the Trinity* concluded with a chapter entitled 'The objections against the Trinity in point of reason answered'. He made no reference to the *Reasonableness of Christianity*, but centred his attack on certain parts of the *Essay concerning human understanding*, particularly that in which substance, according to the bishop, was almost discarded out of the reasonable part of the world. What was particularly embarrassing was that the bishop mixed his criticisms of the *Essay* with an attack on a book, published anonymously in 1696, which had achieved a *succès de scandale*. This was *Christianity not mysterious*, in which reason, not revelation, was made the ground for belief, and in which Christianity was stripped of most of the doctrines to which orthodox anglicans were committed. Its author was John Toland, an able and uninhibited writer who found himself in constant trouble in the course of a remarkable career. Born of Gaelic catholic stock in a remote corner of north-west Ireland he was, as a lad of promise, sent to study at Glasgow University. He later made his way to Holland, where it was intended that he should be trained as a dissenting minister. There he developed a great admiration for Le Clerc. However, his behaviour seems to have been disapproved of by the clergy in Holland. He gave up his study for the ministry and came to England. He had made a more favourable impression on Benjamin Furly, Locke's quaker friend in Rotterdam, who gave him a recommendation to Locke as a 'free-spirited, ingenious man . . . having once cast off the yoke of spiritual authority, that great bugbear and bane of ingenuity, he could never be persuaded to bow his neck to that yoke again, by whomsoever claimed'.[43] However, Locke found Toland too brash and, although he respected his intelligence, was reserved in his association with him. Toland's *Christianity not mysterious* was an able exposition of the reasonableness of Christianity and an open rejection of doctrines that did not carry the authority of reason; it was strongly influenced by the ideas expressed in Locke's *Essay*. Although it was not published until after the *Reasonableness of Christianity*, Toland seems to have been writing *Christianity not mysterious* before that, and it is probable that Locke saw part, at least, of the work in manuscript in the spring of 1695.[44]

In his *Letter to the bishop of Worcester* Locke brushed aside the references to Toland's book and concentrated on parrying the criticism of the *Essay*. The argument continued with further exchanges. Molyneux followed it with obvious interest. He told Locke that he had been discussing it with an ingenious man who thought that the bishop was not directly attacking Locke's views as erroneous but as misused by others, particularly the author of *Christianity not mysterious*. Molyneux himself thought that, though the bishop had taken the appearance of *Christianity not mysterious* as an opportunity for his attack, he was in fact opposed to Locke's views. Molyneux added that he had heard that the author of *Christianity not mysterious* was an Irishman who had apparently been long out of the country, 'for I have not heard of any such remarkable man amongst us'. In his next letter Molyneux wrote that Toland had come over to Dublin and had visited him. He understood that Toland had been a great while abroad, where he was instructed by the great Le Clerc: 'but that for which I can never honour him too much is his acquaintance and friendship to you, and the respect which on all occasions he expresses for you. I propose a great deal of satisfaction in his conversation. I take him to be a candid free thinker and a good scholar. But there is a violent sort of spirit that reigns here, which begins already to show itself against him and, I believe, will increase daily, for I find the clergy alarmed to a mighty degree against him. And last Sunday he had his welcome to this city by hearing himself harangued against out of the pulpit by a prelate of this country.' Locke's reply indicated a very cautious attitude to Toland. He would be very glad if Toland's high opinion of himself did not make him less useful to the world than could be expected of his talents, if rightly directed. Toland had not let Locke know he was going to Dublin; otherwise Locke might have given him an introduction to Molyneux, 'which I am now not sorry I did not'. He hoped Molyneux would be kind to Toland, but left it to his prudence to decide how that kindness should be shown.[45] Molyneux answered that Locke's hints about Toland matched his own apprehensions. Toland had been imprudent and had roused much opposition by his way of talking on serious problems in coffee shops. His habit of constantly referring to Locke as his patron and friend made many who criticised Toland also criticise Locke. At the same time Molyneux looked on Toland as a 'very ingenious man' and was anxious to help him, particularly in view of Locke's recommendation. He added that there was much curiosity as to why Toland had come to Ireland. He had no employment and yet appeared to be provided with money. Locke replied that his recommendation of Toland was only as a man of parts and learning for his age; he did not mean that Molyneux should do more for him than his own judgment of the man might warrant.[46]

Toland was fiercely attacked by Peter Browne, a fellow of Trinity College, Dublin, in *A letter to a book entitled Christianity not mysterious*. Browne made a number of criticisms of Locke in the course of his argument, and suggested that Toland was only the spokesman for a secret club that was intent on destroying religion.

Molyneux deplored Browne's personal attack on Toland and, in particular, his proposal that legal proceedings be taken against him. Molyneux thought it most undesirable that civil courts should be judges of religious doctrine. Toland's book was indicted by a grand jury in Dublin, 'not one of which . . . ever read one leaf in *Christianity not mysterious*'.[47] The book was also debated in the Irish house of commons where it found some members, among them presumably Molyneux himself, to defend it. But the champions of orthodoxy were too strong for the liberals; the book was ordered to be burned by the common hangman and Toland to be arrested and prosecuted. Toland, faced with this threat and the demands of his creditors, made a hasty departure.

William King, bishop of Derry, wrote to Molyneux about some passages in Locke's *Reply to the bishop of Worcester,* expressing surprise that Locke found a contradiction between certainty and faith, certainty being the perception of the agreement or disagreement of two ideas. King thought that this left very little certainty in the world and came near Toland's proposition that authority or testimony is only a means of information, not a ground of persuasion. King suggested that perhaps his disagreement with Locke was about terms, and that if he had carefully read the *Essay concerning human understanding* he might have resolved the difference, 'but I have neither opportunity, leisure, or inclination to do so, and believe a great part of the world to be in the same circumstances with me'. This opened the way for Molyneux to point out the passages in the *Essay* that would have resolved the bishop's difficulty if he had read it 'more carefully and throughout'. He sent Locke the bishop's letter and a copy of his reply as a sample of Dublin opinion: 'I wish you may not say that it resembles our mountains and bogs in being barren and useless'. However, he was sure that he and King were such good friends that this difference of opinion was not likely to cause ill feeling. Locke thanked Molyneux for his reply to King: he thought King must have passed his objections to the bishop of Worcester who had used almost the same words. When Locke's correspondence was published King's letter was included with the heading 'from the bishop of ——'. King was very angry that his private letter to Molyneux should have been published without his permission.[48]

Locke often expressed a wish to meet Molyneux in the flesh, and several abortive plans were made for Molyneux to go to England. But it was not till the last year of Molyneux's life that the meeting eventually took place. In the spring of 1693 Locke bemoaned the distance that separated them: he would gladly have had Molyneux's criticisms of *Thoughts concerning education,* then in the press. In the summer of that year he regretted that Molyneux was not near enough to examine the treatment of power in the *Essay.*[49] Towards the end of 1694 he returned to the subject: 'will you not pardon so lawful a desire in one that loves you if I ask Shall I never have the happiness to see you in England?' Molyneux replied that he had intended to make the journey in the summer of that year particularly to meet Locke. But the state of his health was such that he doubted whether he would be fit to travel. He had tested his strength by a journey in Ireland, apparently to Castle Dillon, and was so tired out that he gave up the idea of travelling to England that summer. He was ill again in the winter and could not make plans for the journey. But he assured Locke that as soon as he was really well he would come to see him: 'there being nothing I so earnestly covet as the personal acquaintance of one for whom I have so great a respect and veneration'. Locke replied that much as he wished to see Molyneux he could never forgive himself if the journey should harm his delicate friend: even if Molyneux made the journey safely Locke would be so ashamed of having subjected him to the ordeal that he would not enjoy the visit. But he would be delighted if some other urgent business should bring Molyneux to England.[50] Locke does not seem to have ever thought of going to see Molyneux in Ireland, a journey that he would have found no less taxing.

What Locke wanted was someone with whom he could discuss his ideas: meditating by oneself was never so good as discussion 'with a knowing, judicious friend who carries about him the true touchstone, which is love of truth in a clear-thinking head'. Molyneux replied that he also regretted the distance that separated them: if providence had not such happiness in store for him as a meeting with Locke he would have missed the greatest temporal good his mind was ever set on. Locke answered that a meeting with Molyneux was the most earnest of all his desires: 'my decaying health does not promise me any long stay in this world; you are the only person in it that I desire to see once and to converse some time with before I leave it'.[51] Molyneux next told Locke that he had thoughts of going to England in the spring or summer of 1696, but that would depend on whether parliament was to be in session. Locke welcomed the idea, but told Molyneux not to pitch his expectations too high: 'come then, but come with this resolution that you will be content, that shall make up to you all those fine things which you imagine beforehand in a man whom you will really find a plain, honest, well-meaning man who unbiassedly seeks truth, though it be but a very small part of it he has yet discovered'. He was afraid that

Molyneux had formed too glowing a picture of him and that he would 'unavoidably fall many degrees in your esteem when you find me come so much short of what you expected'.[52]

The Irish parliament had only token meetings in 1696, but Molyneux's hopes of going to England that year were not realised. He told Locke that his private affairs and public duties made it impossible. As a consolation for his disappointment he hoped to have a portrait of Locke. Thomas Molyneux had married a daughter of Dr Ralph Howard, a prominent Dublin physician. Her eldest brother Hugh, who was now twenty-one, was a promising portrait painter, who subsequently established a considerable reputation. Molyneux had heard that there was a picture of Locke at Churchhill's bookshop. If it was a good likeness he proposed that Howard should copy it; otherwise he asked if Locke would be willing to sit to Howard. Locke replied that Howard had called on him and that he thought him a 'very pretty young gentleman'. He agreed to sit for his portrait, modestly hoping that the skill of the painter would 'make amends for the meanness of the subject, and a good pencil . . . make the painted representation of more value than the real substance'. When the picture was finished Locke was not sure that it showed him as he would like Molyneux to see him: perhaps it was the thought that the picture could bring their actual meeting no nearer that made him look grave.[53] Howard took a considerable time to send the picture to Molyneux, who did not get it until the spring of 1697. However, Molyneux was very pleased with it and thought the artist had shown extraordinary skill. He hung the picture in his dining room and told Locke that Molesworth, 'who is a hearty admirer and acquaintance of yours', had remarked that his visits to Molyneux's house were really expressions of devotion to Locke's portrait. Strangely, the picture of Locke handed down in the Molyneux family bore the more prestigious name of Michael Dahl, painted 1696.[54]

VII

PUBLIC LIFE

FROM the time that Molyneux began to correspond with Locke in 1692 he became heavily involved in political, administrative, and legal work, which diverted him from the scientific interests that had previously occupied so much of his attention. He was already concerned with public affairs as joint surveyor-general and as a commissioner for army accounts.[1] In 1692 he became a member of the Irish parliament, was re-elected in 1695 and remained a member till his death in 1698.

The Irish parliament was closely modelled on that of England. There was a house of lords, presided over by the lord chancellor, consisting of temporal peers and of the bishops of the established church, the Church of Ireland. The bishops formed a much larger proportion of the attendance at the Irish house and exerted more influence than they did in England. The house of commons consisted of two members for each of the thirty-two counties, two members each for the boroughs (117 of them, large and small), and two members for the University of Dublin, making a total of 300. Membership, as a result of a recent English act, was restricted to protestants, but in Molyneux's time catholics were still allowed to vote. The parliament's legislative powers were limited by Poynings' law, which had been enacted by the Irish parliament of 1494-5 and prescribed that no bill should be introduced that had not been approved by both the Irish and the English councils. The Irish parliament had the power to reject bills, but could not make amendments; if a bill was to be enacted it must be in the exact form in which it had passed the great seal of England. This restriction was resented by some members, and the practice had already begun of initiating legislation in the Irish house of commons by 'heads of bills'; draft legislation which the Irish government was asked to convert into regular bills for transmission to England.[2]

The members of the house of commons were mostly country gentlemen who had acquired estates as a result of the confiscations of the sixteenth and seventeenth centuries. There were some representatives of older stock, Gaelic and Norman, who had become protestant. Merchants (some of whom were dissenters), lawyers,

and officials made up the balance. Although the house mainly consisted of post-reformation settlers from Britain, it was proud of its
long traditions which were traced back to the early days of the
Norman conquest, and there was much insistence on formalities
and privilege. A reminder of medieval history was a book, published
in 1692 and edited by Molyneux's brother-in-law, Bishop Anthony
Dopping, entitled *Modus tenendi parliamenta in Hibernia*. This was
a tract describing a parliament with powers and procedure similar
to those of its English counterpart. It was believed to be of the time
of Henry II, but was probably of the fourteenth century. The manuscript had come into the possession of Sir William Domville,
Molyneux's father-in-law, and the tract was later used by Molyneux
in the *Case of Ireland*.

The two university representatives were elected by the provost,
fellows, and scholars of Trinity College, Dublin. On 17 September
1692 they unanimously chose William Molyneux and Sir Cyril
Wyche, who had been secretary to Ormond and was now again
secretary to the lord lieutenant, Henry, Viscount Sydney. At the
same time Wyche was given an LL.D. and Molyneux an M.A.[3] The
provost was St George Ashe, and it may be presumed that his
influence was decisive in the choice of Molyneux, his friend and
fellow-philosopher.

Parliament met on 5 October, and the commons were in an angry
mood. Protestants had suffered much in the conflict between
Jacobites and Williamites, and they resented the fact that the war
had ended in a settlement—the treaty of Limerick—that secured, or
appeared to have secured, estates and privileges to a large number
of the Irish catholics who had taken James's side. In addition there
were ugly rumours of maladministration of the property that had
been seized from the Jacobites by the government and was alleged
to have enriched corrupt officials. King William had promised to do
his best to have the treaty of Limerick ratified by the Irish parliament.
But protestant hostility was so great that the English government
did not then dare to send over a bill for the purpose. The treaty
remained as Banquo's ghost and affected the attitude of the commons
to other questions. The most important of these questions related
to money bills, measures that had been proposed by the two govern-
ments without prior consultation with the house of commons.

On 27 October the commons resolved, without a division, that it
was the sole and undoubted right of their house to prepare 'heads
of bills' for raising money. The next day they rejected one of the
government's money bills, recording that the reason for the rejection
was that the bill 'had not its rise in this house'. This was followed on

5 November by the rejection of the mutiny bill, which provided for
the control of the army, and the presentation of a report that alleged
gross maladministration of the forfeited property. This was too
much for the executive. The parliament was prorogued and subsequently dissolved. Sydney, the lord lieutenant, delivered a celebrated rebuke, no doubt the composition of Sir Cyril Wyche, in
which he made a public protest against the proceedings of the
commons as a breach of Poynings' law and an infringement of the
royal prerogative.[4] Molyneux's name does not appear in the proceedings of this short and stormy session. But it seems that he
supported the government against its critics. This is at first sight
surprising in view of his commitment to government by consent of
the governed. But he evidently distinguished between legislation by
the English parliament, which gave no choice at all to Irish citizens,
and the operation of Poynings' law, which had been passed by an
Irish parliament and gave that parliament the right to reject bills
proposed from England, though not the right to amend them or
initiate their own bills. He may also have been influenced by his
colleague and friend, Sir Cyril Wyche, who was of course committed to the policy of the lord lieutenant. Molyneux has recorded
that the government was pleased with his conduct during the
session, and that before it ended the lord lieutenant offered him an
appointment as a commissioner for forfeited estates. His version of
the affair was that he was put off by the unsavoury reputation that
the forfeiture commissioners had acquired and refused the appointment on the ground of poor health. However, he was a member of
the commission for a few months from November 1692. When the
commission was reorganised in April 1693 he told the lord lieutenant
that his health was much impaired and that his doctors had told
him that nothing but English air could do him any good. He was
allowed to resign but did not then go to England. He noted that his
conduct in parliament had also pleased the university, which in July
1693 made him a doctor of laws.[5]

The Irish parliament did not meet again for nearly three years
during which the administration carried on with the permanent
hereditary revenue. Sydney was recalled, and the government was
in the hands of a troika, Sir Cyril Wyche and William Duncombe,
who were tories and officials rather than politicians, and Henry,
Lord Capel, who was a strong whig politician, anti-catholic and in
favour of toleration for dissenters. There were continual disputes
until Capel, who represented his colleagues as showing undue favour
to catholics, contrived to oust them and become sole governor with
the title of lord deputy. He was confident of his ability to manage

parliament, and a general election was accordingly fixed for the summer of 1695. Molyneux was again chosen by the university, his colleague being Richard Aldworth, who was secretary to Capel. The university evidently wanted to have friends at court to watch their interests. Parliament met on 27 August. Just before it opened Molyneux wrote to Locke: 'the university has done me the honour to choose me as one of their representatives; and though I cannot pretend to do them any great service, yet it shall not be for want of constant attendance on their business, which will take up most of my time till the session is ended'.[6] This, the second parliament of William's reign, outlasted Molyneux's life, and he was kept fully occupied during its sessions in 1695 and 1697. He wrote only one short letter to Locke during the sessions of parliament.

Although Capel managed to get his financial measures passed, insisting on the government's right to initiate one money bill but allowing the commons to initiate a second, the parliamentary session of 1695 was far from harmonious. There was strong party rivalry. The church party were against toleration for dissenters and supported the lord chancellor, Sir Charles Porter, who had been a signatory of the treaty of Limerick and was accused by Capel of favouring catholics. Capel's party supported his policy of toleration for dissenters and anti-catholic legislation. The church party were strong enough to block toleration for dissenters and to prevent the impeachment of Porter, but some penal legislation was passed, restricting education for catholics and preventing them from carrying arms without a licence. A list of members, marked with symbols for pro- and anti-Capel, shows that Molyneux supported Capel's government.[7] He seems to have had friendly personal relations with Capel, to whom he mentioned Locke's name: 'who thereupon expressed himself with the utmost respect and esteem for you'.[8]

Locke, who was at this time preoccupied with the reform of the coinage, sent Molyneux a copy of *Some considerations of the consequences of the lowering of interest, and raising the value of money,* which he had published anonymously in 1691. He told Molyneux 'you may give it to whom you please . . . but pray do not give it to anybody in my name. . . . And however you are pleased to make me a compliment in making me the author of a book you think well of, yet you may be sure I do not own it to be mine till you see my name to it.'[9] In fact, Locke soon afterwords revealed his authorship of *Some considerations* in a pamphlet that he published under his own name at the end of December 1695 with the title *Further considerations concerning raising the value of money.* He also put his name to the second edition of *Some considerations,* published (as the first part of *Several papers relating to money, interest and trade, &c.*) in the following year. It appears that Locke also sent Molyneux a paper containing his official answer to the English lords justices' request for his views on the currency question.[10] Molyneux thought that Locke's original treatise, *Some considerations,* might be too long for Lord Capel, a hard-pressed governor, to read, and that something shorter would be more suitable. The anonymous paper that he gave to Capel was evidently Locke's answer to the English lords justices. Locke's characteristic style betrayed the authorship, and Capel quizzed Molyneux on the subject: 'all the world knows Mr Locke's way of writing and, if I may guess, I believe the paper you gave me a few days ago came from Mr Locke'. Molyneux protested that he was under an obligation to conceal the author's name, but Capel had no doubts: 'I am sure it is his and will put his name to it and lay it up among my choicest papers'.[11] A paper that Molyneux himself subsequently wrote, 'Concerning the raising of the coin in Ireland' argued strongly against fixing too high a rate for the Irish coinage and was evidently influenced by Locke's *Further considerations.* Capel, who had raised the value of the coinage in May 1695, did not take Locke's advice, and the rate was not lowered until 1701.[12]

Molyneux's name appears frequently in the journals of the 1695 session, and it is evident that he was a very active member. The proposed impeachment of Porter raised questions of precedent, and Molyneux was named as one of the principal members of the committee appointed to search the records. He was also selected to present reports from committees on procedure for conferences between the two houses, and on a bill for transferring the archiepiscopal see from Tuam to Galway. His legal knowledge was evidently respected, and during the session he was appointed a master in chancery. Capel noted that he had appointed Molyneux on Porter's recommendation, which suggests that Molyneux had, characteristically, been able to maintain good relations with both sides. The salary of a master in chancery was only £20 a year, but it was a position of prestige and would attract legal business.[13] In the middle of 1696 Capel died. The interim arrangements for government gave a prominent position to Porter, a development that intensified political passions until the end of the year, when Porter himself died. Molyneux deplored the political tension: 'we are now under a most unsettled government and our eyes are fixed on England for relief'.[14]

The new government, appointed early in 1697, consisted of a Huguenot soldier and an ineffective English aristocrat. The Huguenot was Henri Massue de Ruvigny, earl of Galway, who had distinguished himself in the Irish war of 1689-91 and had later been commander of the forces in Ireland. He enjoyed William's confidence, but was looked at askance by catholics, who were afraid that he would persecute them as a reprisal for the sufferings of the Huguenots.[15] The new lord chancellor was John Methuen, a member of the English parliament who had been envoy to Portugal and was later to conclude the Methuen treaty, by which Portugal agreed to take English woollens in exchange for customs concessions on Portuguese wines.

Parliament reassembled on 27 July 1697, and the policy of the government, actively promoted by Methuen, was to obtain belated ratification of the treaty of Limerick, sweetened by anti-catholic legislation. The most notable part of this legislation was an act for the banishment of bishops, other clerical dignitaries, and members of religious orders. The programme was strongly objected to by Bishop King, who was one of a group of lay and spiritual lords who protested that the so-called ratification of the treaty of Limerick was fraudulent. They succeeded in throwing out a bill for the protection of the king's person on the ground that it required catholics, under severe penalties, to take an oath that was against their conscience.[16] It may be presumed that Molyneux supported the government's programme in 1697. He is frequently mentioned in the journals of the session as a member of committees and reporter of bills.

Molyneux told Locke how pleased he was at Methuen's appointment: 'all moderate and good men, I find, are very well pleased at it'. He asked Locke to recommend him to Methuen: 'being one of the masters in chancery here 'tis natural to covet the favour of him under whom I am to act'.[17] Locke had no opportunity of himself speaking to Methuen, but he asked a friend to recommend Molyneux: 'and I promise myself, from thence, that you will find Mr Methuen will be as desirous of your acquaintance as you are of his'.[18] Methuen showed himself friendly to Molyneux, who for his part thought that Methuen had made a very good beginning. The relationship was made all the easier as Methuen appointed as his chaplain Ezekiel Burridge, Molyneux's friend and the translator of Locke's *Essay*. Methuen, Bartholomew van Homrigh (father of Swift's Vanessa) and Molyneux were appointed joint guardians of the young Lord Woodstock and managers of his affairs in Ireland. Woodstock was the son of Hans Willem Bentinck, earl of Portland, who had long been King William's right-hand man. To reward the father's services, and to avoid drawing too much attention to the reward, William had granted to Woodstock the enormous estate in County Cork that had been forfeited by Donough MacCarthy, earl of Clancarty, who was one of James's supporters. An indignant English parliament was later to cancel this and other royal grants of Irish land.[19]

A pressing problem that engaged the attention of both Locke and Molyneux related to Irish textiles. It had long been English policy to regulate the Irish woollen trade so as to reserve Irish wool for the English market and prevent it going to foreign competitors. Previous legislation on the subject had been reinforced in 1662 by an act of the English parliament declaring it to be a felony to export wool from Ireland to foreign countries.[20] There had not been the same objection to the export of Irish woollen cloth, which had traditionally been limited to rough friezes which did not compete with the English cloth trade. But in the closing years of the seventeenth century more refined cloth, termed 'new drapery', was being made in Ireland and exported to the Continent on a small but growing scale. This excited the suspicions of the English cloth merchants, and a campaign was launched to prohibit the export abroad of Irish woollen cloth. A leading part in this campaign was taken by a Bristol merchant, John Cary, author of the widely read *Essay on trade,* published in 1695. In the section that treated of Ireland Cary expressed strong disapproval of the advancement of the Irish trade in woollen cloth. He argued that any increase in the export of Irish cloth would adversely affect the English trade. Ireland should keep to agriculture. If it must have a manufacture let it be linen. To give greater publicity to these opinions Cary extracted the section on Ireland, and a much shorter section on Scotland, and published them separately under the title *A discourse concerning the trade of Ireland and Scotland, as they stand in competition with the trade of England.*

The policy of discouraging the Irish woollen trade had traditionally been matched by efforts to encourage the linen trade, which had reached significant proportions in Ulster, but had not taken root in the rest of the country in spite of various attempts to develop it. After Locke became a member of the board of trade in April 1696 he entered into discussions with Molyneux on the subject. The weight of their correspondence leaned towards the encouragement of linen rather than the discouragement of wool, although Locke produced some ideas for making the latter as painless as possible. In September he asked Molyneux for an account of the linen manufacture in Ireland, with his opinion on how it could be developed. He suggested that the royal navy could be supplied with flax and hemp products from Ireland.[21] Molyneux described recent attempts to develop the linen trade, all of which, outside Ulster, had collapsed.

He thought Ireland, and especially the north, admirably suited for linen. He added that some of his Armagh tenants produced excellent diapers for household use. He made it clear that he was alive to the state of feeling in England about Irish textiles: 'England, most certainly, will never let us thrive by the woollen trade; this is their darling mistress, and they are jealous of any rival. But I do not see that we interfere with them in the least by the linen trade. So that that is yet left open to us to grow rich by, if it were well established and managed.'[22]

In March 1697 the campaign against the Irish woollen trade was taken into the English parliament where a bill was introduced to prevent the export abroad of Irish woollens; it lapsed with the prorogation of parliament. The board of trade pursued the question of Irish textiles and took evidence from some members of the Irish parliament, who advised that the woollen industry should be replaced by linen. Locke's scheme, which was accepted by the board, was that the Irish parliament should impose a graduated scale of duties on imports essential for the woollen industry, and at the same time give fiscal and other encouragement to the linen industry. In the meantime the heads of a bill for encouraging linen had been introduced in the Irish parliament by James Hamilton of Tullymore, a County Down landowner. This was a very mild measure which the Irish government proposed to strengthen by adding fiscal provisions on the lines of Locke's proposal. Hamilton objected to any change involving money being made by the government, apparently regarding it as contravening the 'sole right' of the commons to initiate money bills.

In accordance with Poynings' law the Irish council turned Hamilton's 'heads' into a regular bill and sent it to the English council. Molyneux wrote to tell Locke that the bill was with the English council and sent him a copy of Hamilton's 'heads'. He remarked that it was not the complete solution but was 'a fair beginning to so great an attempt'. The Irish commons had been given a copy of the board of trade report, but at too late a stage to amend Hamilton's draft. Molyneux added that Hamilton greatly admired Locke and had specially given his draft for Locke's benefit.[23] The English council referred the bill to the board of trade, which made some amendments. But Locke thought the fiscal provisions were inadequate and refused to sign the report. The English council evidently agreed and refused to approve the bill, which accordingly lapsed. Locke still hoped that something could be done for the linen manufacture and asked Molyneux to discuss the board of trade report with Hamilton and consider whether it was suitable or whether a bill on those lines would be impracticable and likely to fail: 'I mightily have it upon my heart to get the linen manufacture established in a flourishing way in your country'.[24] Molyneux answered that he had hopes that Hamilton would go to England and explain the situation to Locke: 'he is master of the whole mystery (and that I cannot pretend to be), and would have discoursed you most satisfactorily concerning it'.[25] From the fate of the linen bill that was rejected by the Irish parliament after Molyneux's death it appears possible that the mildness of Hamilton's proposals came from his sense that the church party was not in favour of substantial help for linen, which they regarded as a dissenter interest.

When the English parliament met again at the end of 1697 the campaign against the Irish woollen trade was renewed with greater strength. On 14 December the commons heard a petition from Exeter merchants complaining that the increase in the Irish woollen trade had greatly diminished the English trade and praying for relief. The house ordered a bill to be brought in, to be prepared by Sir Edward Seymour and Sir John Elwell. It also resolved that a committee be appointed to consider the general question of English and Irish trade, with the object of improving the former. Seymour and Locke's friend Edward Clarke were on this committee. A month later Seymour presented a bill to restrain the export of Irish woollens to foreign parts.[26] Seymour was a formidable figure, the leader of a group that Defoe nicknamed 'Seymskeyes western empire', with particularly strong influence in the clothing counties of the west country.[27] The apprehensions aroused in Ireland by the proceedings at Westminster were multiplied by the publication at the end of 1697 of a pamphlet entitled *A letter from a gentleman in the country to a member of the house of commons in reference to the votes of the 14th instant,* [14 December 1697]. This asserted that Ireland was a most dangerous rival to England, and in particular to the English woollen trade: 'by the cheapness and large staple of their wool, the multitude of Irish spinners, and cheapness of their work they are in a fair way of being more than rivals in our woollen manufactures'. It bears all the signs of a design to provoke a confrontation between the two countries, and produced an angry reply, by 'Sir F. B.', who was probably Sir Francis Brewster, a well-known entrepreneur and member of the Irish parliament, and who had been called into consultation with the English government on the Irish textile problem. Bishop King was also highly critical. A correspondent in England had told him that the *Letter from a gentleman* was the work of John Toland, an ascription which he found convincing, 'since it has so great a mixture of wickedness and thoughtlessness in it . . . [and]

Mr Toland has reason to be angry at Irish parliaments, since they made the kingdom too hot for him.'[28]

Seymour's bill did not find favour with the English government. King William was anxious not to have trouble in Ireland. He followed Methuen's advice and was 'convinced he ought to protect Ireland in the house of commons and hath actually spoken to most of the considerable persons to come into such measures as may hinder the bill about the woollen manufactures'.[29] Methuen, who sat in the commons as member for Devizes, made strenuous efforts to oppose Seymour's bill, but he thought that 'nothing can be done by the Irish to avert such action without an effective bill to establish an Irish linen industry'.[30] The king was of the same opinion and considered that, as the Irish parliament had failed to get a linen bill on to the statute book, the only alternative was to have an English act to regulate the Irish linen industry. Methuen was sure that this would be strongly opposed by 'our friends in Ireland'.[31] As an indication that serious efforts were being made to encourage the production of Irish linen Methuen introduced a Huguenot to the king. This was Louis Crommelin who, on promise of substantial government aid, undertook to introduce up-to-date techniques to Ireland and did, in fact, establish a celebrated linen manufacture at Lisburn, County Antrim.[32] In spite of the opposition put up by Methuen, Robert Molesworth, and Lord Coningsby, a former lord justice of Ireland, the woollen bill passed the commons on 21 February 1698. However, Methuen had great hopes that it would be held up in the lords and continued to lobby against it. He was, however, afraid that his efforts would be frustrated by 'the zeal and diligence of the gentlemen of Ireland . . . who are every day pub- lishing books and papers not suiting with this climate'.[33] An example of this zeal was a pamphlet entitled *Some thoughts on the bill depending before the right honourable the house of lords for prohibiting the exportation of the woollen manufactures of Ireland,* which argued that the effects of such a prohibition would be to destroy the protestant interest in Ireland. But much more trouble was caused by the publication, in April 1698, of Molyneux's *Case of Ireland's being bound by acts of parliament in England, stated,* which was a direct challenge to the authority of the English par- liament. Methuen's efforts to persuade the house of lords to hold up the woollen bill were successfully exerted against the powerful influence of Lord Chancellor Somers, who was already disturbed by the constitutional implications of a legal battle between Bishop King of Derry and the Londoners, to whom that city had been granted by James I. Methuen convinced some influential English

lords that a revised linen bill would soon be brought before the
Irish parliament.[34] This argument seems to have been effective.
Seymour's woollen bill was allowed to lapse with the prorogation of
the English parliament in July. Before that the lords had made an
address to the king. They asked him to declare to his subjects in
Ireland that the growth of their woollen manufacture was looked
on with great jealousy, and if not timely remedied might occasion
very strict laws, meaning English laws, for the total prohibition of
the industry.[35] The commons also addressed the king: 'we cannot
without trouble observe that Ireland, which is dependent on and
protected by England in enjoyment of all they have . . . should of
late apply itself to a woollen manufacture to the great prejudice of
the trade of this kingdom . . . the consequence whereof will
necessitate your parliament of England to interpose to prevent the
mischief that threatens us unless your majesty by your authority
and great wisdom shall find means to secure the trade of England
by making your subjects of Ireland to pursue the joint interest of
both kingdoms'. William's response was conciliatory: 'Gentlemen,
I shall do all that in me lies to discourage the woollen manufacture
in Ireland and to encourage the linen manufacture there and to
promote the trade of England'.[36]

THE CASE OF IRELAND

T HE independence of the Irish parliament had been asserted by the Anglo-Norman colonists of medieval times. The most notable example of the claim was in 1460, when the parliament called by Richard, duke of York, declared that Ireland was and always had been 'freed of the burden of any special laws of the realm of England, unless they had been accepted by the lords and commons of Ireland'.[1] The claim of the Irish parliament to be the exclusive legislative authority for the country was challenged in the seventeenth century with increasing frequency. In 1634 when parliament had rejected government bills the viceroy, Lord Wentworth (later earl of Strafford), had pssed the bills as 'acts of state', showing scant regard for Irish susceptibilities. After Strafford's fall his highhanded action was condemned by the parliament, of which both catholics and protestants were members. They had an eloquent spokesman in Patrick Darcy, a catholic lawyer from Galway, whose *Argument* asserted that the inhabitants of Ireland were a free people, to be governed only by the common law and by statutes made by the Irish parliament.[2] The outbreak of violence in Ireland in 1641, followed by the English civil war, led to a series of acts and ordinances of the English parliament for the regulation of Irish affairs. The most conspicuous was the 'Act for the speedy and effectual reducing of the rebels in . . . Ireland' (the adventurers' act of 1642), which invited subscriptions for the suppression of the rebellion on the security of lands to be forfeited in Ireland. This was seen as a flagrant breach of constitutional rights, and was the subject of a protest to Charles I by a catholic delegation which demanded that an act be passed declaring that the Irish parliament was a 'free parliament of itself, independent of, and not subordinate, to the parliament of England', and that the people of Ireland were immediately subject to the crown.[3]

The question came up again in the closing stages of the commonwealth regime, this time from the protestant side. A convention which met in Dublin early in 1660 to settle the arrangements for the restoration of the monarchy included in its proceedings a declaration that the time-honoured right of holding parliaments in Ireland to pass laws and grant subsidies had been invaded by the commonwealth authorities who had imposed taxes on Ireland. The convention was assisted by a disquisition on the traditional independence of the Irish parliament, drawn up by William Domville, Molyneux's father-in-law. It argued the case for the exclusive legislative authority of the Irish parliament with a wealth of legal precedent from medieval times. Much of Domville's disquisition was later incorporated in Molyneux's *Case*.[4] During the reign of Charles II several acts applying to Ireland were passed in the English parliament, representing a further encroachment on the Irish constitutional position. The legislative independence of Ireland was upheld by the 'patriot parliament' summoned in Dublin in 1689 by James II, which passed a declaratory act stating that no act of parliament passed in England, even if it mentioned Ireland, should in any way be binding on Ireland unless it was passed into law by the Irish parliament. It was also prescribed that no appeals from Ireland should be made to the English house of lords.[5] With the defeat of James II and the victory of William III the proceedings of the patriot parliament were declared null and void by parliament in both England and Ireland, and the declaratory act of 1689 was a dead letter. However, its substance was in line with the views of many protestants, though it was politically impossible for them to support their case with the aid of Jacobite legislation.

Molyneux was of one mind with his father-in-law in upholding the traditional privileges of the Irish parliament, of which he was proud to be a member. The English bills for the restriction of the Irish woollen industry were a clear threat to those privileges, and the spirit in which the bills were debated showed that there was much English hostility to the Irish parliament. The *Letter from a gentleman in the country* . . ., which Bishop King's informant had attributed to Toland,[6] had sought, presumably at the prompting of the opposition in the English parliament, to extend the conflict beyond commercial issues to the constitutional relations between the two countries. It had declared that Ireland was a most dangerous rival to England and should not be allowed control of her own government or trade. She should have no parliament and all her trade should be regulated by acts of parliament in England. In the detailed refutation of the *Letter* which King sent to his friend, Sir Robert Southwell, the bishop expressed sentiments very similar to those that Molyneux was to express in the *Case*: if Ireland was to 'be governed by the parliamentary law of England we shall like it very well provided we be all represented in the English parliament . . . I take all power that is not with consent of the subject to be arbitrary'.[7] These views reflected King's further interest in the jurisdictional aspects of the constitutional relations between England and Ireland. As bishop of Derry he had become involved in a lawsuit with the London companies who owned large estates in Ulster. King won his case in the Irish house of lords, but early in 1698 the Londoners appealed to the English house of lords, which eventually held that the Irish lords had no jurisdiction, and gave the verdict to the Londoners.[8] Molyneux was personally concerned in helping the bishop with legal precedents, and he saw the proceedings as a further attack on the rights of the Irish parliament.[9]

This was the context in which Molyneux spent the early months of 1698 in producing his most celebrated book, *The case of Ireland's being bound by acts of parliament in England, stated*. He offered as justification for venturing to challenge the proceedings of the formidable English parliament, when others remained silent, his belief in that parliament's sense of justice and his conviction that if its members were fully informed of the Irish case they, as asserters of their own liberties and rights, would refrain from encroaching on those of a neighbouring country. He claimed that he was acting not only on behalf of Ireland but of mankind generally: 'it is the cause of the whole race of Adam that I argue; liberty seems the inherent right of all mankind'.[10] He made a somewhat ingenuous disclaimer of any interest in the wool trade or in the litigation between the bishop and the Irish Society: 'I think I am as free from any personal prejudice in this cause as 'tis possible to expect any man should be that has an estate and property in this kingdom and who is a member of parliament therein. I hope therefore 'tis a public principle that has moved me to this undertaking'.[11]

The political situation in England made rapid composition essential if Molyneux was to get a hearing. His task was greatly facilitated by Domville's disquisition, which was a convenient source for the medieval precedents that take up the greater part of the book. He incorporated many passages from Domville word for word. His other major source was Locke's *Two treatises of government*, the influence of which can be seen in various parts of the argument and the language of which is sometimes closely followed. Molyneux paid tribute to 'an incomparable treatise' and embarrassingly went on to say: 'this discourse is said to be written by my excellent friend John Locke Esq'. In a correction of his original draft he attempted to honour Locke's desire for anonymity by adding 'whether it be so or not, I know not'. But Locke cannot have relished the introduction of his name.[12]

Molyneux's case was argued on two levels: the historical status of the Irish parliament, and representative government as a natural right. The greater part of the book is a legalistic survey of history and precedent. It draws heavily on Domville's disquisition, but Molyneux himself had made an elaborate study of parliamentary proceedings in a survey that extended beyond the restoration and up to his own day.[13] The parts of the book that present the argument from natural rights owe much to Locke. The survey of precedents is an intimidatingly detailed blend of legal learning and fictitious history. The reputation of the book depends on its eloquent assertion of natural rights.

Molyneux traced the origins of the Irish parliament to Henry II, who accepted the voluntary homage of the Irish kings, nobility and clergy and who in turn was said to have allowed 'the freedom of holding of parliaments in Ireland as a separate and distinct kingdom from England'.[14] For the guidance of parliament he was said to have given the *Modus tenendi parliamenta in Hibernia* which, with some adjustment for Irish conditions, was parallel to the English *Modus,* said to have been granted by William the conqueror. Molyneux was at pains to show that Henry's dealings with Ireland were by agreement and not the result of conquest. Henry II's alleged use of the title *Conquestor Hiberniae* appeared to imply that Ireland was a conquered country, but Molyneux argued that the people of England would 'take it very ill to be thought a conquered nation in the sense that some impose it on Ireland'—on the ground that William I was called the Conqueror. In fact, he went on to say, England could much more properly be said to have been conquered by William than Ireland by Henry. Molyneux then distinguished between an unjust conquest, which gave no right to force men to part with their birthright of being governed by consent, and a just conquest, which gave the conqueror absolute power over the lives and liberties of those who had opposed him.[15] Even if it was argued that Ireland had been conquered, either by Henry II or subsequently in the course of rebellions, he contended that conquest might properly restrict the liberties of actual rebels but not those of their descendants. In any case the penalties of conquest could not properly be used against those of British descent who had assisted in the suppression of rebellions. Here Molyneux made the extraordinary statement that the great majority of 'the present people of Ireland are the progeny of the English and Britons that from time to time have come over into this kingdom, and there remains but a mere handful of the ancient Irish at this day'.[16] He thus apparently relegated the greater part of the population to the category of non-persons. He may have been thinking of the 'political nation', the men of property. Molyneux's discussion of conquest owed much to Locke's second treatise, to which he referred his readers: 'they that desire a more full disquisition of this matter may find it at large in an incomparable *Treatise concerning the true original, extent, and end of civil government,* chapter 16'.[17]

Molyneux continued with an analysis of the legal position, citing numerous English acts that were not applied to Ireland until adopted by the Irish parliament. These included English acts expressed as applicable to all the king's subjects and dominions. Molyneux maintained that such expressions could not bind Ireland any more than they could bind Scotland. More difficulty was caused by English acts that specifically mentioned Ireland, notably the staple act of Henry VI, which ordered that all wool exported from England or Ireland should be landed at Calais. In a case against the merchants of Waterford the chief baron of the Irish exchequer, overruling a previous decision of his fellow-barons, found that statutes made in England did apply to Ireland. Molyneux contended that this decision was unreasonable and had been so regarded by other commentators. He quoted an English yearbook of Richard II's time which held that Ireland was not bound by English statutes because it did not have knights of parliament in England: he added 'and is not that an unanswerable reason'.[18] Elsewhere he observed that if it was 'concluded that the parliament of England may bind Ireland it must also be allowed that the people of Ireland ought to have their representatives in the parliament of England. And this, I believe, we should be willing enough to embrace; but this is an happiness we can hardly hope for.'[19] These sentiments were then widely shared among the settler community. The passage shows that Molyneux was a champion of the right to representation, but not an Irish separatist. The 'patriots' of the eighteenth century who made a hero of Molyneux did not draw attention to this aspect of his principles, and the passage was omitted from the edition of 1782.

A new situation developed in the seventeenth century when Molyneux admitted that several English acts were effectively applied to Ireland. But he contended that these were innovations of which the people of Ireland complained: 'therefore they ought not to be brought in argument against us'.[20] The most important of such acts was the adventurers' act of 1642, offering forfeitable land to subscribers of money. Molyneux explained that as Ireland was then 'under an horrid intestine rebellion, flaming in every corner of the kingdom' no parliament could be held in Ireland and the only course available was for the parliament of England to intervene.[21] In fact, the Irish parliament had continued to meet. In any case, he contended, the act was a temporary measure as it was superseded at the restoration by the Irish act of settlement. In Charles II's reign there were several English acts that applied to Ireland: an act forbidding tobacco planting, the navigation act that obliged Irish shipping coming from the plantations to put in first at an English port, and an act that made it a felony to send Irish wool abroad. Molyneux asked whether such recent proceedings could be made grounds for depriving a nation of the rights and liberties it had enjoyed for five hundred years.

Bishop King thought that Molyneux should not have admitted that these seventeenth-century acts were binding on Ireland. He maintained that the adventurers' act was aimed at the king, whose prerogative of granting forfeited land was transferred to the English parliament; the navigation act merely fixed the conditions under which trade could be conducted with the English plantations; the tobacco act was ignored; the wool act confirmed an existing Irish act and the penalty it imposed was never inflicted: 'in short I am told there is not one judgement in our country given against the life or property of any subject of Ireland under an English act'.[22]

Molyneux admitted that during the conflict between James II and William III several acts affecting Ireland were passed in England. But he argued that the circumstances were exceptional: 'we cannot wonder that during the heat of a bloody war in this kingdom when it was impossible to secure our estates and property by a regular parliament of our own, we should have recourse to this means as the only [one] which then could be had'.[23] Soon after that war had ended in 1691 an important act was passed in England, prescribing for Ireland the oaths and declaration to be taken by members of parliament and others, which for the first time provided a statutory bar to membership of the Irish parliament for catholics. Molyneux, expressing the protestant point of view, argues that these acts 'were looked upon highly in our favour and for our benefit, and to them as such we have conformed ourselves, But . . . if a man who has no jurisdiction over me command me to do a thing that is pleasing to me, and I do it, it will not thence follow that thereby he obtains an authority over me and that ever hereafter I must obey him of duty'.[24]

Molyneux particularly resented the claim that Ireland was only an English colony and that, as the Roman colonies were governed by the senate's laws so Ireland should be governed by laws made at Westminster. He protested that Ireland was 'a complete kingdom within itself. Do not the kings of England bear the style of Ireland amongst the rest of their kingdoms? Is this agreeable to the nature of a colony? Do they use the title of kings of Virginia, New England, or Maryland?'[25]

In the concluding section of the book the case for representative government was treated as a natural right. Molyneux's argument was taken from Locke's contract theory of government: all men are by nature equal, 'free from all subjection to positive laws till by their own consent they give up their freedom by entering into civil societies for the common benefit of all the members thereof. And on this consent depends the obligation of all human laws.'[26] The claim to legislate without consent was a direct attack on property: 'to tax me without consent is little better if at all than downright robbing me. I am sure the great patriots of liberty and property, the free people of England, cannot think of such a thing but with abhorrence.'[27] He ended with a plea for the preservation of parliamentary rights in an age of absolutism. Parliamentary government, which had once flourished all over Europe, had now almost disappeared: 'our king's dominions are the only supporters of this noble Gothic constitution, save only what little remains may be found thereof in Poland. We should not therefore make so light of that sort of legislature and as it were abolish it in one kingdom of the three wherein it appears, but rather cherish and encourage it whenever we meet it.'[28]

Molyneux took much care over the composition of the book. His style of advocacy has been analysed in a recent appreciation: his assumption that the reader is reasonable, will acknowledge truth once he is reminded of it, and will be convinced by a demonstration of the issues involved; legal texts and precedents are dutifully marshalled, but they are much less important than the appeal to natural law.[29] There are two drafts in the library of Trinity College, Dublin. The first, in Molyneux's hand, appears to be the original draft, with corrections in many places, sometimes toning down what might seem offensive to an English readership. The second copy, in the formal script of a clerk, served as the printer's copy, as the markings on it show. It also has some corrections, most of them in Molyneux's hand. An interesting erasure in the printer's copy is of a passage relating to Scotland: 'and were it to my purpose I could show that it were equally if not more reasonable to make Scotland subordinate to the parliament of England than to make Ireland so, for we know what submission, tribute, homage, and fealty many of the Scots kings have paid to the kings of England in ancient and later times . . .'.[30] Evidently Molyneux decided that he did not wish to add to his difficulties by arousing the wrath of patriotic Scots. The title in the original draft, 'An humble remonstrance to the parliament of England in relation to Ireland', was at first repeated in the printer's copy. But apparently Molyneux thought that 'remonstrance', a term associated with the vocabulary of protest, was likely to give offence. He was not altogether satisfied with the alternative title that took its place, 'The case of Ireland's being bound by acts of parliament in England, stated and argued'. The last two words were then eliminated, and so the book was given what became its familiar title.

He dedicated the book to the king, praising him for his intervention to rescue England and her fellow-nations from arbitrary power. Of the three kingdoms Ireland had most reason to be grateful for being raised from the depth of misery and despair to a prosperous and flourishing condition. He entreated the king as the common indulgent father of all his countries not to permit the eldest of his children, because the strongest, to encroach on the possessions of the younger. Molyneux asked Bishop King for help in getting the book presented to William III, a request that the bishop clearly found embarrassing. However, he did not like to refuse and passed the request to his legal adviser Francis Annesley, a member of the Irish parliament, leaving it to his discretion what to do.[31] Annesley evidently thought it would be ill-advised to do anything, and the book was not presented to William.

It appears that the book was completed by 26 March, the original date assigned to the preface. Molyneux changed this to 8 February and it has been suggested that the change was made to avoid a charge that it referred to matters that were under examination by the English parliament. The eighth of February was the day on which the lord chancellor of England presented to the house of lords a collection of records relating to appeals from the Irish court of chancery, which were required in connection with the bishop of Derry's case in the English house of lords; some of the records concerned the question of the independence of the Irish parliament. Molyneux's treatment of this question might have appeared more injudicious if it was seen that the book had been completed after the English lords were apprised of these records.[32]

While the book was in preparation Molyneux made no direct reference to it in his correspondence with Locke, though its theme was touched on in a letter of 15 March: 'the parliament in England . . . bear very hard upon us in Ireland. How justly they can bind us without our consent and representatives I leave the author of the *Two treatises of government* to consider'.[33] Locke replied that he was very concerned for Ireland and wished it well. He would like to discuss the problem with Molyneux, but not by letter: Molyneux should come, well prepared for a personal discussion. But meanwhile if Molyneux was talking to others on the subject Locke's name should not be mentioned.

It was not till Molyneux's book had been printed, in April, that he told Locke about it: he had been moved by the parliamentary proceedings at Westminster to write a book about England's treatment of Ireland. Locke would no doubt think this was a delicate subject, but Molyneux considered that he had handled it 'with that caution and submission' that it ought not to give offence. He had therefore not hesitated to put his name to the book and had 'by advice of some good friends here' presumed to dedicate it to the king. He had despatched some copies to Churchill for presentation to Locke and some of Locke's friends and he invited Locke's opinion, which should be as frank as the opinions Molyneux had given on Locke's books. In spite of his protest that the subject had been treated with discretion Molyneux was obviously nervous about the effect the book would have on the English parliament. He thought it would not be wise to go to England till he saw how parliament took the book or till the end of the session: 'though I am not apprehensive of any mischief from them, yet God only knows what resentments captious men may take on such occasions'.[34]

Locke did not answer this letter but his correspondence with his friend Edward Clarke, one of the members of parliament most active in promoting the woollen bill, strongly suggests that he disapproved of Molyneux's book and apprehended that the book, with its mention of Locke's name, might be used as a means of attacking him. Locke thanked Clarke for promising to see 'that I receive no inconvenience by the indiscretion of a man which mightily surprised me. But as there is no fence against other people's folly, so I think nobody is to answer for other people's follies but they themselves.'[35] Locke's reaction was to be expected. He was well aware of the English parliament's sense of its power and its resentment of any derogation of parliamentary privilege. Apart from this, Molyneux had made the oppression of Ireland by England, and not merely by the parliament, the object of his protest. Locke was very much the Englishman, and several passages in Molyneux's book were calculated to raise his hackles: as he had earlier written to Clarke 'whilst I have any breath left I shall always be an Englishman'.[36]

The contents of the book soon became known to Irishmen in London, who evidently thought it would lead to trouble and wished to dissociate themselves from the views expressed in it. Methuen was reported to have said that they went so far as to complain to the

king, apparently on the ground that Molyneux had been so pre-
sumptuous as to dedicate the book to his majesty, and that William
was naturally very angry and ordered that the author should be
prosecuted.[37] Apart from the presentation copies Molyneux intended to put the book on sale in England, and copies sent over
had a revised title page stating that they were to be sold by Robert
Clavel and A. and J. Churchill, booksellers in London. Methuen,
who thought Molyneux's book was a disaster, succeeded with
Molesworth's assistance in preventing its sale in London during the
parliamentary session. Molyneux seems to have been relieved that
a stop had been put to the sale of the book in England. But in spite
of Methuen's precaution some members of the commons were
determined to raise the question of the book in the house and use
the occasion to attack Ireland and embarrass the government.
Methuen consulted some of the ministry, and it was arranged that
King William should order him to bring the book before the house
and inform it that the king had ordered the author to be prosecuted
and that 'all the gentlemen of Ireland in town did disown the principles of it'. Methuen wrote to Lord Galway that the book 'hath
given us the most trouble and hazarded all our ruin', meaning the
collapse of his plans to block Seymour's woollen bill. He considered
that the book had also a disastrous effect on Bishop King's case, in
which the English house of lords declared that the Irish house had
no jurisdiction.[38]

The book was debated in the commons on 21 May, when Methuen
read out passages which, according to a report of the proceedings,
'deny the dependence of Ireland upon the parliament of England or
that they were bound by laws enacted here, further than they thought
fit themselves'. He assured the house that these opinions expressed
only the views of the author and that the Irish gentlemen were
scandalised by them. In spite of this assurance there was a strong
body of opinion in the commons that Molyneux would not have
ventured to write without the encouragement of others, and that
recent proceedings in the Irish parliament showed that his doctrines
were widely held. The house appointed a committee to examine the
book and to inquire into the proceedings in Ireland that might have
encouraged the author. Locke's friend, Edward Clarke, proposed a
motion that the whole Irish parliament had acted on the principles
set out by Molyneux, and the committee sent for all the bills transmitted from Ireland since the revolution of 1688, 'pretending to find
great faults and breaches of Poynings' law'.[39]

The committee took a month to examine the book and on 22
June 1698 reported that it had found thirty passages 'which tend to

the disowning and denying the authority of the parliament of England over Ireland'. The committee also scrutinised the proceedings of the last session of the Irish parliament. It took particular exception to the heads of a bill for the security of the king's person. This appeared to re-enact a law already passed in England and did so with alterations that purported to restrict the authority of the great seal of England in giving effect to its provisions. Furthermore it referred to the imperial crown of Ireland. Methuen himself was subjected to some criticism for having, as lord chancellor of Ireland, affixed the great seal to bills that were 'derogatory to the rights of the crown of England'.[40]

The house of commons resolved *nem. con.* that Molyneux's book was 'of dangerous consequence to the crown and people of England by denying the authority of the king and parliament of England to bind the kingdom and people of Ireland, and the subordination and dependence that Ireland hath and ought to have upon England as united and annexed to the imperial crown of this realm'. It also resolved that the Irish bill for the security of the king's person 'pretending to oblige the courts of justice and the great seal of England by the authority of an Irish parliament' had encouraged Molyneux to publish. This was followed by an address to the king in which complaint was made of the dangerous attempts of some of his Irish subjects to shake off their dependence on the kingdom of England, revealed by the bold and pernicious assertions in Molyneux's book. The king was asked to give effectual orders to prevent anything of the sort taking place in the future and to punish those who had been guilty of these subversive attempts. William replied that he would take care that what was complained of should be prevented and redressed. He gave instructions on these lines to the Irish government, but the latter took no action to punish Molyneux or those who were said to have encouraged him.[41]

It is commonly thought that the book was ordered to be burned by the common hangman, a legend that added greatly to its reputation among Irish patriots of the eighteenth century. But no such order was recorded in the commons' journals and there is no contemporary evidence that the book was burned. If it had been, the replies to the book could hardly have failed to mention the fact. It seems likely that Methuen's influence was enough to prevent such humiliating treatment. He was sorry for Molyneux and made efforts to prevent 'anything violent against the book or the author'. The commons were disposed to regard Molyneux as an unimportant figure in comparison with the larger body of insubordinate Irish parliamentarians who were the real villains. As Methuen put it: 'as yet we have put off any hurt to Mr Molyneux's book. .... The intention of most angry people is not to be severe against Mr Molyneux but to charge his opinions on all Ireland.'[42] Molyneux himself had no wish to escape in this way and was ready to take full responsibility for his book. Bishop King was informed that the English parliament intended to spare Molyneux but revenge themselves on the kingdom: 'that is a thing he in no way desires and is very unjust'. King thought that the book 'being written by a private gentleman without consulting anybody that I can find' should not have been used to 'justify a public resolution to the detriment of a kingdom'.[43] There was some criticism of Methuen's conduct. It was alleged that he had at first complimented Molyneux on the book and then condemned it.[44] But it seems unlikely that Methuen, who was well aware of how the English parliament would react, should ever have thought it a well-timed publication.

It was not long before replies to the *Case* appeared in England. In the middle of July, Bishop King, who was staying at Bath for his gout, wrote to Annesley that he longed to see the answers to Molyneux's book and asked for copies.[45] Four such answers bear the 1698 imprint, and presumably at least two of them had been published by July.

John Cary, the Bristol merchant who had taken a leading role in the campaign against the Irish woollen trade, was the author of a tract entitled *A vindication of the parliament of England in answer to a book written by William Molyneux of Dublin, Esquire, intituled The case of Ireland's being bound by acts of parliament of England, stated.* The tract, as befitted the author of the *Essay on trade,* took up the economic issue and declared that unless Ireland were controlled by English laws it would destroy the English woollen trade: Ireland and its parliament should be put on the level of 'our other plantations'.[46] But the greater part of the work was a detailed critique of the precedents cited by Molyneux, answering them point by point. Cary explained that he had engaged Molyneux with his own weapons and thrown back those darts which Molyneux had cast at the power of English parliaments.[47] The pamphlet, which Cary dated 16 June 1698, seems to have been first in the field.

The longest, and perhaps the most influential, reply bore the title *The history and reasons for the dependency of Ireland upon the imperial crown of the kingdom of England, rectifying Mr Molineux's State of the case of Ireland's being bound by acts of parliament in England.* The dedication, to the members of the English house of commons, bore the name of William Atwood, a well-known writer on constitutional questions, a strong whig, and a champion of the rights of the English parliament. He later became a controversial chief justice of New York. Atwood met Molyneux on his own ground, matching one series of ancient precedents with another. He turned the myth of the ancestral constitution to the disadvantage of Ireland. The laws of Edward the Confessor were used to counter Molyneux's reliance on the constitution granted to Ireland by Henry II, and their authority was cited for the claim that King Arthur had annexed Ireland. A charter of King Edgar was quoted as including among his God-given possessions 'the greatest part of Ireland with its most noble city Dublin'. Coming to recent times Atwood made the telling point that it was the English parliament that had given Ireland a king in the person of William III. He answered Molyneux's point that taxation without representation was downright robbery by arguing that the right of taxing did not follow from the right of governing.[48]

A third reply, according to its dedication, was not completed until Atwood's book had already appeared. It bore the title *An answer to Mr Molyneux his case of Ireland's being bound by acts of parliament in England, stated, and his dangerous notion of Ireland's being under no subordination to the parliamentary authority of England refuted by reasoning from his own arguments and authorities.* The author presented a copy to Locke, and is identified by the latter's library catalogue as Simon Clement, a London merchant to whom a number of tracts on trade and currency have been attributed.[49] It was dedicated to the 'modern English nobility, gentry, and protestant inhabitants of Ireland', and contained the politically effective argument that Molyneux had based his case on medieval concessions said to have been made to the native Irish and the early settlers, the ancestors of the catholic supporters of James II. The protestants in Ireland—Molyneux's own community—were committed to acceptance of William and Mary as sovereigns by right of the recognition granted to them by the English parliament.

Early in 1699 a fourth reply appeared, which took a completely different stand from that of its predecessors. *Considerations of importance to Ireland, in a letter to a member of parliament there upon occasion of Mr Molyneux's book intituled The case of Ireland's being bound by acts of parliament in England, stated* has been attributed to Charles Leslie. It accepted with wholehearted approval Molyneux's thesis that Ireland was independent of the kingdom, though not of the king, of England up to the end of Charles II's reign. But it argued that Molyneux's case was completely undermined by his acceptance of the English act of 1691 that imposed fresh oaths, including one of allegiance to William and Mary, and a declaration denying catholic doctrine on those who held public positions in Ireland. Molyneux's excuse that this was a voluntary acceptance gave away the whole Irish case. Leslie had been chancellor of the diocese of Down, but as a passionate non-juror had been obliged to give up the office. To him it was the requirement of allegiance to William rather than the repudiation of catholic doctrine that was offensive. The tract urged the Irish parliament to assert itself and disown the authority claimed for English legislation: 'I am sure the longer that Irish parliaments continue to pay obedience to this English act the precedent grows the stronger and works still more towards a prescription'.[50]

The Case, so strongly condemned in England, had no champions in Ireland, where those who had undoubtedly shared Molyneux's views were intimidated by the manifest power of the English parliament, and even in their private correspondence deplored the publication of his book as rash and inopportune. The book appeared destined for oblivion. The leaders of protestant opinion in Ireland for a time decided that their best hope of obtaining redress lay in a union that would give them representation at Westminster and free them from restrictions on their trade. Their thinking was closely in line with that of the Scots, who were also coming to think that union was the only way out of an intolerable situation. The heavy hand of the English parliament continued to be laid on Ireland. Not only was the export abroad of Irish woollens forbidden but titles to Irish land granted by William III were questioned and overturned by the agents of the English commons under the authority of statutes forced upon the crown in a successful bid to drive the remnants of the Whig Junto from office. In the first of Anne's Irish parliaments the house of commons asked her on 20 October 1703 either to restore her Irish subjects to the full enjoyment of their constitution—the exclusive right of legislation—or to grant them 'a more firm and strict union' with her English subjects. The Irish house of lords had passed a similar resolution on 1 October 1703, requesting that such a representation of the condition of Ireland be laid before the queen as should incline her to promote a union.[51]

To these and other resolutions of the kind a negative reply was invariably given. The approach and realisation of union between England and Scotland was contrasted with the neglect of Ireland, and it became clear that such a solution of Irish problems was not to be forthcoming. Swift pointed the contrast in a tract written, but not published, at this time with the title 'The story of the injured lady, being a true picture of Scotch perfidy, Irish poverty, and English partiality'.[52] Union had been an alternative solution put forward by Molyneux, and the contrast between the offer of terms to Scotland and their refusal to Ireland reawakened interest in the *Case,* which was reissued in 1706 with no indication of the printer or place of publication. In 1719 a celebrated case, Annesley versus Sherlock, was the subject of appeal to the British house of lords, which set aside the Irish verdict, a virtual repetition of the bishop of Derry's case in 1698, and which led to the publication of another edition of Molyneux's book, again without the name of the printer or the place of publication. The assertion of the right of the British house of lords to be the final court of appeal for Ireland was given statutory authority in 1720 by a British act that was a crushing repudiation of Molyneux's case. This was the celebrated 'sixth of George I', the declaratory act that both denied the appellate powers of the Irish house of lords and asserted the right of the British parliament to pass laws for Ireland.[53] The declaratory act inspired a fourth edition of the *Case,* this time with a London imprint. Its publication was the first shot in the long struggle to get the act repealed, a struggle in which the Irish patriots of the eighteenth century were to make repeated use of Molyneux's arguments. The next edition, embellished with a portrait of Molyneux, was published in Dublin in 1725 at the height of the controversy over 'Wood's halfpence', the contract to coin halfpence for Ireland granted by the London government to a Wolverhampton iron-monger who was alleged to have made an inordinate profit by the use of base metal. The opposition was led by Dean Swift, whose Drapier letters were effective propaganda and established him as the 'Hibernian patriot'. In the fourth letter he broadened the argument beyond the halfpence by denying that Ireland was a 'depending kingdom'. He continued: 'it is true indeed that within the memory of man the parliament of England have sometimes assumed the power of binding this kingdom by laws enacted there, wherein they were at first openly opposed (as far as truth, reason, and justice are capable of opposing) by the famous Mr Molineaux . . . but the love and torrent of power prevailed. Indeed the arguments on both sides were invincible. For in reason all government without the consent of the governed is the very definition of slavery, but in fact eleven men well armed will certainly subdue one single man in his shirt.'[54]

The next edition of the *Case,* published in Dublin in 1749, appeared at a time of political excitement stirred up by Charles Lucas, a radical doctor who devoted his life to a vigorous battle against arbitrary government and had issued a series of addresses on the rights and privileges of the Irish parliament. He referred to 'that strenuous asserter of truth and liberty, that just pattern of loyalty, that faithful friend and subject of his king, and sincere lover of his country, our Molyneux'.[55] The publisher's advertisement stated that instead of 'meeting with the approbation Dean Swift and others of our patriots thought it deserved' the original edition of Molyneux's book had been condemned to the flames, a martyrdom that was to be claimed repeatedly for it. The advertisement added that Swift thought so highly of the book that 'he was often heard to say that it ought to be written in letters of gold'.[56]

With growing tension between Britain and the American colonists from the stamp act crisis of 1765 to the outbreak of hostilities in 1775 much attention was paid on both sides of the Atlantic to the similarities, and differences, in the cases of Ireland and America. Westminster claimed the right to legislate in both cases, but its claim to tax the American colonies had not so far been extended to Ireland. Molyneux's book, which was directly concerned with these matters, was used in the propaganda of the colonists as well as of the Irish patriots, and several new editions were published. Copies of the book found their way into the libraries of Thomas Jefferson and James Madison.

The 1770 edition was published in London by John Almon, radical journalist and friend of John Wilkes. It omitted the dedication to the king and had a new preface which referred to the 'cruel treatment' of the American colonists, and also gave an emotive account of the circumstances in which Molyneux's book had originally appeared: the citizens of Ireland 'saw their independence unjustly violated, their trade wantonly distrained, and Mr Molyneux's modest, dispassionate, irrefragable proof of the rights and liberties of his native countrymen profanely burned by the hangman'. Benjamin Franklin sent a copy of this edition to a Boston friend, referring to the preface and adding 'our part is warmly taken by the Irish in general, there being in many points a similarity in our cases'. Samuel Adams referred to the book in a letter to the *Boston Gazette*: 'we shall esteem the arguments of so sensible, and it may justly be added so learned, a gentleman as Mr Molyneux, especially as he had the approbation of his friend Mr Locke, to be valid'.[57] Adams, of course, was mistaken in supposing that Locke approved of Molyneux's arguments. He would, however, have based his estimate of Molyneux's sense and learning on the *Familiar letters* or on their reproduction in Locke's *Works*.

An edition published in Dublin in 1773 had another preface in which the American crisis was reviewed and Lord North attacked for using Irish pensions to secure a 'mercenary majority' in the British parliament. If he became all-powerful in this way he could treat both Irish and Americans as 'horse, asses, and slaves at his pleasure'.

The edition of 1776 was published in Belfast, where the greatest enthusiasm for the American struggle was to be found. A preface recommended the book as 'highly useful to be read and understood by all who glory in the freedom and independence of this kingdom, which is here asserted from history, from law, from policy, and from nature'. Molyneux had written it at a time when the English parliament had attempted to 'blast a part of that general liberty restored to the empire on the accession of William III . . . The same lust of domination, which hath led them to encroach on the constitutional rights of our fellow subjects in America, may, if their attempt should succeed, lead them to desire to bind Ireland by their laws "in all cases whatsoever".' The last phrase was taken from the declaratory act of 1766, the assertion of British parliamentary power that was the American equivalent of the declaratory act imposed on Ireland in 1720. The implication was that success in America would be followed by the taxing of Ireland.

The relevance of Molyneux's book was obvious to those who took part in the movement for constitutional reform that dominated the Irish scene in the closing years of the American war, and effective use was made of it in parliamentary oratory. Henry Flood declared 'the case of Ireland originally stated by the great Molyneaux, and burned at the revolution by the parliament of England, is not now afraid of the fire; it has risen from that phoenix urn, and with the flames of its cradle it illuminates our isle'.[58] A Dublin paper printed an ode to Molyneux, in which he was hailed as a patriot 'who singly dared to stem his country's doom . . . braving a monarch's frown in freedom's cause'.[59]

When the demand for constitutional reform was granted and the declaratory act repealed in 1782 Grattan made a triumphant speech in the course of which he invoked the ghosts of former patriots: 'spirit of Swift, spirit of Molyneux, your genius has prevailed. Ireland is now a nation.'[60] The occasion was marked by yet another edition, this time published in Dublin, which significantly omitted the words in which Molyneux had referred to union with England as a 'happiness we can hardly hope for'. The preface explained that the edition had been planned to add strength to Irish demands. The granting of those demands seemed to make it unnecessary, but publication was decided on so that 'Irishmen being put in possession of the best arguments in support of their liberty may always be as attentive to its preservation as they have been virtuous and spirited in the obtaining it'.

The reforms of 1782 admitted the specific claims put forward by Molyneux, the denial of the right of the Westminster parliament to legislate for Ireland and the establishment of the Irish house of lords as the final court of appeal. These rights had been claimed by Molyneux for an all-protestant parliament, and it was for an all-protestant parliament that Grattan obtained them in 1782. The reforms were in fact short-lived, vanishing with the act of union of 1800, which balanced the loss of Irish legislative independence by the grant of Molyneux's alternative, the 'happiness of union'. But it was Molyneux's demand that Irish laws should be made by a representative parliament that struck the imagination of Irishmen of all creeds, and historians of differing political beliefs have given general commendation to him as a liberal patriot.

LAST DAYS

IRONICALLY, the political crisis that contributed to Molyneux's decision to write the *Case,* which proved so distasteful to Locke, renewed Locke's desire for an early meeting with Molyneux, so that they might discuss such problems in person. Early in April 1698 he wrote to Molyneux: 'I meet with so few capable of truth, or worthy of a free conversation, such as becomes lovers of truth, that you should not think it strange if I wish for some time with you for the exposing, sifting, and rectifying of my thoughts . . .'[1] Molyneux answered that he had been thinking of coming to England for his health, but that Locke's letter had made him forget his health: 'the desire of seeing and conversing with you has drained all other expectations from my journey, and I am resolved to accomplish it, let what will come on it . . . I shall therefore embrace you, God willing, as soon as ever the parliament of *England* rises. I fix this period now, not so much in expectation of our chancellor's arrival, as on another account'.[2] While Methuen was in England the great seal of Ireland was entrusted to commissioners, of whom Molyneux was one. He had previously told Locke that this was the reason why he could not then come to England, but evidently his presence on the commission was not essential.[3] 'Another account' was, of course, the publication of the *Case,* which he now for the first time divulged to Locke. He knew that he would run the risk of being arrested by an aggrieved English house of commons if he came within its jurisdiction.

Bishop King went to Bath early in July to take the waters for his gout, and Molyneux had planned to travel with him. But by the time the bishop left Dublin Molyneux had not had news of the end of the English parliamentary session, and he did not venture to make the crossing. In the middle of July King wrote to Annesley: 'Mr Molyneux would have come over with me if he durst, and now that parliament is risen I expect him very soon, though I believe he will go by London and come from thence hither'.[4] Evidently King's disapproval of Molyneux's publication did not make any breach in their friendship. Shortly after parliament had risen Locke wrote to Molyneux to say that he had just come to London and hoped to see Molyneux soon: 'I long mightily to welcome you hither, and do remit to that happy time abundance that I have to say to you'.[5] Locke had clearly made up his mind that nothing should cloud the long-awaited meeting. There is no definite evidence as to when Molyneux reached London, but it seems to have been about the beginning of August. He spent five weeks with Locke and was back in Dublin on 15 September.[6] There is a baffling lack of information about his visit: what he and Locke talked about and how they spent the time during which Locke was not occupied with the board of trade. The board met daily from Monday to Friday, and during Molyneux's visit Locke missed only one day.[7] That was 19 August, which was a Friday and with the Saturday and Sunday may have given Locke the opportunity of taking Molyneux to see his friends the Mashams at Oates. Molyneux was delighted to make their acquaintance and later wrote to Locke: 'that part thereof [i.e. of his visit to Locke] especially which I passed at *Oates,* has made such an agreeable impression on my mind that nothing can be more pleasing'. During August the board was much concerned with the Irish linen question, and it may be presumed that Locke discussed it with Molyneux.[8]

When in London Locke stayed with his friend Robert Pawling, comptroller of the stamp office, who was then living 'over against the Plough in Little Lincoln's Inn Fields'.[9] During the visit Locke arranged for Molyneux's portrait to be painted by Sir Godfrey Kneller. Molyneux had left for Dublin before the portrait was ready. Locke noted in his journal for 21 September that he had 'paid Sir Godfrey Kneller by his servant that brought the picture £8, which with the £8 I paid him before is £16'.[10] On 15 November a correspondent informed Locke that neither his portrait nor that of Molyneux was yet finished.[11] Apparently the picture brought by the servant was the portrait for which Locke had sat to Kneller in 1697 and for some reason was returned to Kneller. Locke later remarked that Molyneux's name had been inscribed on the back of his portrait, which he regarded as a wise precaution to secure future identification.[12] It is not known what eventually happened to the portrait of Molyneux or whether it reached his family. If it passed to Samuel's widow it might well have gone out of the possession of the Molyneux family together with Molyneux's books and papers. Sir William Wilde thought that Kneller was the painter of the portrait of Molyneux in Trinity College, Dublin.[13] That, however, was by Robert Home, who was commissioned by the college in 1783 to do a series of portraits.[14] It is not known from what source Home gave his picture the eager innocent expression that contrasts with the intimidating figure in the 1725 edition of the *Case*. Thomas Molyneux's grandson thought sufficiently well of Home's picture to use it to illustrate his history of the family.

While he was in London Molyneux took an active part in trying to arrange a compromise between Bishop King and the London companies, working in collaboration with King's counsel, Francis Annesley.[15] He also went round the bookshops, as appears from his signature in several 1698 publications. There is, however, no evidence that he attended a meeting of the Royal Society.

When he got back to Dublin Molyneux wrote to express his appreciation of Locke's hospitality: 'I cannot recollect through the whole course of my life such signal instances of real friendship, as when I had the happiness of your company for five weeks together in *London*. 'Tis with the greatest satisfaction imaginable, that I recollect what then passed between us, and I reckon it the happiest scene of my whole life'.[16] This suggests that controversy was buried and that differing opinions on the relations between England and Ireland were avoided in favour, perhaps, of philosophy. Locke answered with equal cordiality: 'I lived with you and treated you as my friend, and therefore used no ceremony nor can receive any thanks but what I owe you doubly both for your company, and the pains you were at to bestow that happiness on me. If you keep your word, and do me the same kindness again next year, I shall have reason to think you value me more than you say, though you say more than I can with modesty read.'[17]

But within a month of his return to Dublin Molyneux was dead. He died on 11 October, aged forty-two, after an illness of only two days. It appears that the strain of the journey had brought on his chronic kidney trouble.[18] He was buried in St Audoen's church, Dublin, where a monument with a Latin inscription marked his grave.[19] The monument was later removed, but Molyneux is still commemorated in what remains of the church by an inscription in English in which he is styled 'the man whom Locke was proud to call his friend'.

When he got the news Locke wrote to Thomas: 'I have lost in your brother, not only an ingenious and learned acquaintance, that all the world esteemed, but an intimate and sincere friend, whom I truly loved, and by whom I was truly loved'. He asked Thomas if there was any way in which he could be of service to him or to William's son, Samuel: 'I cannot think myself wholly incapacitated from paying some of the affection and service that was due from me to my dear friend as long as he has a brother or a child in the world'.[20] In his reply Thomas said that William during his short

illness had several times spoken of Locke with great respect. He
had with his own hand written a clause in his will: 'I give and
bequeath to my excellent friend *John Locke,* Esq. author of the
Essay concerning human understanding, the sum of five pound to
buy him a ring in memory of the value and esteem I had for him'.[21]

Molyneux's last year was full of drama: the publication of the
book that was to make him famous, the traumatic experience of
severe condemnation by his king and by the English parliament,
the excitement and pleasure of the long-awaited visit to Locke. It is
not easy to imagine how he would have developed had he lived.
He had said his say on the independence of the Irish parliament
and had been made painfully aware of the pitfalls of such a controversial subject. His interests had earlier moved from science to
philosophy. In both phases he had owed much to an outstanding
personality ready to correspond at length with him. Without
Flamsteed he could not have made his contributions to astronomy
and optics. His philosophical ideas were developed under the
stimulus of Locke, and it is doubtful whether he would have derived
the same stimulus from Berkeley. Molyneux had a strong radical
streak, unusual in the conservative society of protestant Dublin. He
found a congenial companion in Robert Molesworth, who had
acquired fame, or notoriety, by his bold attack on the authoritarian
government of Denmark and became the patron of Toland. A
modern commentator has associated Molyneux, Molesworth, and
Toland with Locke as 'commonwealthmen', heirs of the puritan
revolution.[22] The characteristics ascribed to commonwealthmen are
opposition to arbitrary power in state or church, the toleration of
differing opinions, and the belief that laws should be made with the
consent of the governed.

It is difficult to assess Molyneux's attitude to the church. Some
of his best friends were bishops, but he distinguished between the
liberals and the illiberals on the bench. He appears to have borne all
the signs of a conscientious Christian, but his Christianity was that
of Locke, rational and with a minimum of dogma. He was clearly
attracted by Toland, but the author of *Christianity not mysterious*
was writing in the role of a Christian, and we do not know how
Molyneux would have regarded the later deist or pantheist. In an
autobiographical letter to his brother, Molyneux several times
adopted a specifically Christian attitude to his troubles: it pleased
God to give him Christian submission to the tragedy of his wife's
blindness; when his first child died it pleased God to blast all his
hopes and joy in him; when civil commotion banished him to
Chester in 1689 he was comforted by entire reliance on God and by

diverting his thoughts with his usual studies.[23] A sign of heterodoxy may be found in the attraction he felt for Fontenelle's *Entretiens sur la pluralité des mondes*. He said he was so mightily pleased with the subject and the author's way of managing it that he got his cousin, the younger Sir William Domville, to translate it.[24]

Molyneux combined high intelligence with naivety and an insensitivity to the effect his opinions and actions might have on others. But he was thoroughly likeable, with great charm and without guile, and much was forgiven him, though Flamsteed's patience was eventually exhausted. In contrast to the timid Locke, Molyneux showed courage in putting his name to the *Case,* which was regarded as dangerous and subversive by English politicians, and in Ireland was deplored as indiscreet and harmful by many of those who privately shared his opinions and whose cause he had endeavoured to promote. But many of those who regretted the publication of the book tried to protect the author from what they considered to be the natural consequences of his folly, and they bore him no ill will.

His interests were very diverse: mathematics, astronomy, optics, natural history, philosophy, and the structure of society. He showed great energy in their pursuit, but was prone to switch from one line of inquiry to another. He was ambitious both for himself and for his family, of which he was proud and to which he was eager to add lustre. His endurance of recurring pain, his patient concern for his wife in her affliction, his care of his motherless son were the characteristics of a warm-hearted and strong personality. His relations with his father and brother were harmonious and affectionate, and marked by a common bent for intellectual inquiry and experiment. He was clearly not regarded as of the stature of Locke or Berkeley, but his mental power, the frankness with which he expressed his opinions, his organising capacity, and his industrious pursuit of what he set his hand to had a significant effect on the intellectual and political life of his own day, and made an unexpectedly persistent impact on later times.[25]

Appendix A

THE MOLYNEUX PROBLEM

M OLYNEUX'S 'jocose problem' of the blind man, the sphere, and the cube secured attention in many countries as a result of its inclusion in the second edition of Locke's *Essay concerning human understanding*.[1] What answer should be given to the question has long been argued about and still attracts the interest of philosophers and psychologists. Molyneux's answer was that the blind man on gaining his sight would not be able to distinguish sphere from cube by looking at them, although he had previously learned to distinguish them by touch. Locke expressed his agreement with this answer, adding some variations of his own. They were contradicted by Leibniz, who had read Locke's *Essay* in Pierre Coste's French translation and discussed Molyneux's problem in the course of his critique of the *Essay*.[2] The critique takes the form of a dialogue in which Philalethes presents Locke's ideas and Theophilus those of Leibniz himself. Philalethes recounted to Theophilus the problem set by 'the learned Mr Molyneux, who employs so profitably his excellent genius in the promotion of the sciences', and asked Theophilus for his opinion on it. Theophilus replied that the problem, which appeared quite curious, really required time for an answer, but as he had been asked for an immediate opinion he would venture to say that if the formerly blind man knew that the objects were a sphere and a cube he would be able to tell them apart without touching them. He would be able to distinguish them by the principles of reason, united with the sense-knowledge with which he was already provided by touch, even though he might at first be dazzled and confused by the novelty of the situation. Leibniz's reason for answering Molyneux's question in the affirmative was that geometry—in this case the difference between an object without angles and an object with eight corners— could be learned both by touch and, more usually, by sight. In both cases the ideas were the same, though for a blind man unable to see and for a paralytic unable to touch the images would be different. He speculated about the ideas of a man born blind and cited some cases of the deaf and dumb who had gained hearing and speech and gave interesting accounts of their previous conceptions.

Leibniz suggested that Locke was not so far from his own position as might at first appear. Locke, after initially agreeing with Molyneux that the answer was No, added that 'at first sight' the blind man would not 'with certainty' be able to distinguish sphere from cube—reservations that corresponded to Leibniz's own hesitations. But it was to be expected that Locke and Leibniz would come down on different sides of the fence. Their epistemologies were opposed: Leibniz believed in innate ideas; Locke rejected them, and so did Molyneux. They made experience the basis of knowledge. Locke's qualification—'at first sight'—may mean no more than that the formerly blind man must learn by experience, as a normal infant must learn.

In a tract entitled *Anti-scepticism* Henry Lee observed that Locke's negative answer 'served his turn to prove that nature does less and experience more for our gaining knowledge than we are aware of'. Lee disagreed and asked whether 'there be not in nature a necessary connection between a certain motion upon the organs of touch and a certain perception, and a certain figure at the bottom of the eye, and that same perception'.[3]

Berkeley discussed the problem in his *New theory of vision* and answered it in the negative: 'a man born blind would not at first reception of sight think the things he saw were of the same nature with the objects of touch or had anything in common with them . . . so that he would not call them by the same name nor repute them to be of the same sort with anything he had hitherto known'. Berkeley, in fact, thought the man would not understand the question, which would appear to him 'downright bantering and unintelligible'; he would not be able to refer tangible ideas to the new visual ideas. Berkeley made a complete separation between the sense of touch and the sense of sight. He, as Locke had done, made the qualification 'at first reception of sight', which would not debar the man from learning by experience to make the distinction between sphere and cube.[4]

In the same year, 1709, that Berkeley's *New theory* was published a cataract operation was performed in London by a surgeon named Grant, which was described in the *Tatler*.[5] According to the description the patient, a young man of twenty, was greatly moved by the experience. He studied the surgeon from head to foot and then looked at himself, apparently making a comparison. He thought their hands were exactly alike, apart from the instruments, which he took to be part of the surgeon's hands. He was emotionally upset by the voice of his lady love and eagerly observed her appearance as she spoke. But in talking to her he 'showed but very faint ideas of anything which had not been received at the ear'. It is doubtful how authentic this description is, and it does not directly answer Molyneux's question. But the ability to recognise and compare hands would be more compatible with an affirmative than with a negative answer. Berkeley does not appear to have seen the account of the case at the time, in spite of his eagerness to obtain such evidence. Four years later his friend Sir John Percival wrote to him: 'you have now an opportunity of gratifying one piece of curiosity which I have heard you are very inquisitive about when on this side, I mean the surprise of a person born blind when made to see. One Grant, an oculist, has put out an advertisement of his art this way, with whom I believe you will find satisfaction in discourses.'[6]

Francis Hutcheson, who came from County Down to teach in Dublin while Berkeley was there, thought that Molyneux and Locke were both wrong. Hutcheson thought that the formerly blind man by taking a side view would discover the equal uniform round relievo of the sphere and distinguish it from the outlines of the cube. For Hutcheson visual and tangible extension were the same idea, though our perceptions of them were distinct. If they were different ideas 'one who had only the idea of tangible extension could never apprehend any reasonings formed by one who argued about the visible, whereas blind men may learn mathematics'. Hutcheson's view was similar to Leibniz's, but independently arrived at: Leibniz's *Nouveaux Essais* was not published till 1765.[7]

In 1728 a more famous operation was performed by William Cheselden, who was a fellow of the Royal Society and surgeon to the queen. His report was published in the *Philosophical Transactions*.[8] The patient was a boy of thirteen or fourteen 'who was born blind or lost his sight so early that he had no remembrance of ever having seen'. According to Cheselden's report the boy 'thought no objects so agreeable as those which were smooth and regular, though he could form no judgment of their shape or guess what it was in any object that was pleasing to him: he knew not the shape of anything nor one thing from another, however different in shape or magnitude; but upon being told what things were whose form he before knew from feeling he would carefully observe that he might know them again, but having too many objects to learn at once he forgot many of them'.

Voltaire, who was in England at the time, later observed that the experiment confirmed all that Locke and Berkeley had foreseen. He said that it decisively confirmed that what we saw was not the immediate result of the angles formed in our eyes: the immediate object of sight was coloured light. The rest we perceive only by time and experience. We learn to see as we learn to speak and read.[9]

James Jurin, who was both a physician and a mathematician, considered (1738) that Cheselden's experiment showed clearly that the perception of the convexity of a globe and the angularity of a cube was a matter of judgment and not of sight, a doctrine well demonstrated by Locke and Berkeley. But Jurin did not think highly of Molyneux's 'famous problem', nor did he think that Molyneux himself had solved it. Jurin found a marked difference between Molyneux's statement of the case and that of Locke. The answer given by Locke qualified his negative by saying that the formerly blind man could not make the distinction with certainty at first sight, limitations that were not to be found in Molyneux's question. Jurin argued that Molyneux would allow the man to look again and again and observe the objects from every side by walking round them and also to use his reason: these aids would enable him to tell which was globe, which cube, without touching them. Jurin's contention, in which he claimed to have the support of Robert Smith, professor of astronomy and mathematical philosophy at Cambridge,[10] rather unreasonably assumes that Molyneux meant to allow all that he did not specifically exclude. Locke's response does not give the impression that he wished to differentiate his view from Molyneux's.

Condillac discussed the Molyneux problem in two of his works. The earlier was his *Essai sur l'origine des connaissances humaines* (1746), in which he held that the reasoning of Locke's account was based on the false assumption that the impression of a flat coloured circle was all that was conveyed to the soul, and that if we saw a globe as convex it was only because by the experience of touch we had accustomed ourselves to judge it as such. He thought that Locke had no evidence for this assumption: 'for myself when I look at a sphere I see something other than a flat circle'.[11] Condillac concluded that the formerly blind man would distinguish globe from cube by sight because he would recognise the same ideas that he had already gained by touch. But could he be sure that what he saw as a globe was the same as what touch told him was a globe? Would he know that what appeared a globe to his eyes was not a cube when handled? Condillac thought that the Cheselden case, for which he quoted Voltaire, did not confirm the views of Locke and Berkeley: those who observed the behaviour of the man born blind when the cataracts were removed were hoping to have their preconceptions confirmed and did not suspect that there might be other reasons than those imagined by Locke and Berkeley.

Condillac returned to the discussion in his *Traité sur les sensations* (1754) in which he admitted that his previous treatment in the *Essai*, in which he had maintained that the eye naturally judged shapes and other forms of extension, was prejudiced. In the *Traité* he introduced the famous statue, which was at first endowed only with the sense of smell, to which the other senses were successively added. He now held that it was only the sense of touch that could give knowledge of extension and that touch taught the other senses to judge external objects. He thought that Molyneux in posing his problem had grasped only part of the truth. In introducing the factor of size and requiring the globe and cube to be 'nighly of the same bigness' Molyneux had presupposed that sight without the aid of touch could give different ideas of size; if that was the case there was no reason for Molyneux and Locke to deny that sight without the aid of touch could distinguish shapes. Condillac maintained that it was Berkeley who was the first to think that sight alone could not make judgments of extension. He followed this up with a detailed exposition of the Cheselden case and listed a number of precautions to be observed in recording the experiences of those newly endowed with sight.[12]

Diderot discussed the Molyneux problem in his *Lettre sur les aveugles* (1749). He examined Condillac's treatment of the problem in the *Essai sur l'origine des connaissances humaines* and observed that Condillac's reasoning led to the conclusion that either the formerly blind man could see nothing or that he would see the difference between the sphere and the cube. Diderot agreed with Condillac in thinking that Molyneux's proviso about the size and material of the sphere and the cube was gratuitous if, as Molyneux and Locke held, there was no essential connection betwen sight and touch. According to Diderot Condillac thought that if, in spite of being able to distinguish sphere and cube, the man hesitated in naming them it must be for complicated metaphysical reasons, an excessively free rendering of Condillac's actual words.

Diderot himself thought that the man would not be able to see shapes and distinguish objects: he also asked whether, immediately after the operation, he would be able to see at all. This led Diderot to a discussion of the Cheselden case, on which he remarked that for a long time the youth could not distinguish the sizes or shapes of objects. He thought, however, that experience would enable the youth to distinguish shapes by sight without the aid of touch. Diderot compared the ability of different types of people to make such a distinction. The uneducated would, once their eyes had recovered, see objects clearly but would not be able to compare sensations of sight and touch. Others would make the comparison and, mentally running their hands over the objects they saw, would distinguish them as circle and square without knowing why, an apparent contradiction of Diderot's negative answer to Molyneux's question. A philosopher, using his reason, would also be able to distinguish sphere and cube, seen as circle and square, as soon as he could see clearly at all. But more complicated shapes would present greater difficulties. The philosopher would also be uncertain of the connection between the sensations of sight and touch and would say: 'this object seems to be a circle and this one a square, but I have no guarantee that they will be the same to touch as to sight'. A mathematician would say that if he were to believe his eyes one of the figures was a circle and one a square, for only on this supposition could he apply the techniques he had already devised to make the distinction. He might show some hesitation in this reasoning and speculate whether the same figure could appear as a square to the sighted and a circle to the blind, but he would soon make up his mind that this was not so. The mathematician in whom Diderot was particularly interested was Nicholas Saunderson, who in spite of being blind from the age of one became professor of mathematics at Cambridge. Saunderson had devised an ingenious system of squares and pins to enable him to make his calculations, and Diderot described it in detail. It is probable that he learned about Saunderson from the latter's *Algebra* (Cambridge, 1740). But Diderot cited a work said to have been printed in Dublin as his source: 'The life and work of Dr Nicholas Saunderson, late Lucasian professor of the mathematics in the university of Cambridge, by his disciple and friend William Inchlif Esq'. This work appears to have been fictitious; the Dublin attribution may reflect the city's reputation in the scholarship of vision.[13]

A letter in the *Gentleman's Magazine* for 1752 over the name 'Anti-Berkeley' argued that a formerly blind man would already have known that his hand was divided into fingers and on gaining his sight would at once see the division into fingers. Though his mind would be affected in a new and different way yet the similarity of the impressions gained by touch and by sight would be enough to 'conclude before he touched his hand that the thing he now saw was the same which he had felt before and called his hand'. The writer asserted that Molyneux's solution of the problem of the sphere and the cube, though acquiesced in by so great a man as Locke, was probably wrong.

Thomas Reid, the Scottish philosopher, discussed the Cheselden case in *An inquiry into the human mind* (1764). He noted that

Cheselden's patient on becoming able to see could perceive little or nothing of the real shape of objects, 'nor could he discern that this was a cube, that a sphere'. From this he deduced that at first the youth's eyes would give him almost no information about external objects. Those objects would present the same appearance to him as they do to us 'and speak the same language, but to him it is an unknown language'. This suggests that Reid would have answered Molyneux's question in the negative, which is surprising as Reid, unlike Molyneux and Locke, was a believer in innate ideas. Sir William Hamilton in his edition of Reid's works (1846) held that Reid had misinterpreted Cheselden, whose account of the youth's efforts to observe meant that he must have seen the difference between objects of different shapes, even though he could not identify and name by sight the objects that he had previously identified and named by touch. A sphere and a cube would make different impressions on him, but he probably could not assign to each its name. This again amounts to a negative answer to Molyneux's question, though Hamilton added that the slightest consideration would enable a person already acquainted with the figures 'to connect them with his anterior experience and to discriminate them by name'.[14]

Joseph Priestley, philosopher and chemist, discussed Molyneux's 'famous problem' in *The history and present state of discovery relating to vision, light and colours* (1772). He agreed with Jurin's affirmative answer: even though sight would not give the man the idea of anything more than flat shapes they could be distinguished from one another, so that a circle could be known from a square, though a square might not be distinguished from a cube.[15] Priestley's answer presupposes that the man could relate the three-dimensional perception familiar to him by touch to his newly acquired two-dimensional perception.

During the nineteenth century, as cataract operations became more common, a number of experiences of the blind from birth were recorded, and these records formed the basis of discussion by philosophers. The discussions were chiefly concerned with the relation of sight and touch, and there were fewer attempts to give specific answers to Molyneux's question than there had been in the eighteenth century. One such attempt was made in *Sight and touch: an attempt to disprove the received (or Berkeleian) theory of vision,* published in 1864 by Thomas Kingsmill Abbott, Fellow of Trinity College, Dublin, and later professor of philosophy in the university. He disagreed with the answers given by Molyneux, Locke and Berkeley. His argument was that if the formerly blind man was informed that one of the objects now visible to him was a sphere and the other a cube and he already had by touch an idea of the difference he would be able to make the identification. The notion of a straight line, which he had already acquired by touch, would also be obtainable by sight: 'when the eye traverses an edge of the cube it comes to an abrupt stop and the look must turn in a different direction several times in the circuit, and a similar change occurs when the cube is handled. But the globe gives to both senses the idea of a continuous uniform outline.' He examined a number of recorded cases, but neither the records nor Abbott's reflections on them afford ground for definite conclusions. He made the interesting point that on account of Molyneux and Locke English surgeons made a practice of using a sphere and a cube to test the perceptive powers of their patients. Subsequently Abbott found a case that appeared both to be satisfactorily recorded and to provide a conclusive answer. This was a cataract operation performed in 1903 by a Dr Ramsay on a man blind from birth. On the second day that the patient got out of bed he was shown a ball and a toy brick, told what they were, and asked if he could tell them apart. He looked at them for several minutes, moving his head from side to side and backwards and forwards; at the same time his fingers moved nervously as if trying to feel the objects in imagination. At length he named them without hesitation. Dr Ramsay formed the opinion that the patient had answered correctly because he was able to compare what he saw with an imaginery tactile impression. Abbott concluded that his case contradicted the differing views of Molyneux, Locke and Berkeley. He thought that Locke on his own principles, which made judgment part of the perceptive process, ought to have answered in the affirmative; in Berkeley's words: 'for it is no more but introducing into his [the patient's] mind by a new inlet an idea he has already been well acquainted with'.[16]

The German philosopher, Ernst Cassirer, laid great stress on the importance of the Molyneux problem in his *Philosophie der Aufklärung* (1932). He regarded it as a focus for the whole range of eighteenth-century problems in epistemology and psychology. He thought that the Cheselden case completely vindicated the negative answer that Berkeley had given on theoretical grounds: the case verified the theory that there was no inner affinity between the data of touch and sight, and that the relation between them was founded on nothing more than on their habitual connection.[17]

Of recent years there has been a marked interest in the problem, often associated with psychological inquiry into the problems of vision and particularly directed to recordings of the experiences of the blind on acquiring sight. The latest extended study of the problem is by a Cambridge experimental psychologist, M. J. Morgan, whose *Molyneux's question* was published in 1977. Morgan linked the views of Locke, Berkeley, and the French philosophers to the concerns of modern psychology. Much of his book consists of summaries of the eighteenth-century literature, with particular attention to Condillac and Diderot. Morgan extended his field to cover more general theories about the nature of perception, such as those of Lotze and Kant.

Students of philosophy have also continued to puzzle over Molyneux's question. It has special interest for Berkeley scholars, foremost among them A. A. Luce, who considered the Molyneux problem of capital importance to Berkeley when he was designing his theory of vision. Luce observed that Berkeley's commonplace book had fifteen entries that raised questions about the blind who acquired sight. The earliest entries, which dealt with the heterogeneity of sight and touch, raised questions in connection with the Molyneux problem. Luce considered that it was this problem that stamped on Berkeley's imagination the idea that we do not touch and see the same object: unless the sense of the space to sight and of the space to touch were distinct the answer given by Molyneux and Locke would be wrong.[18] H. M. Bracken has discussed the problem in *Berkeley* (1974), calling it a philosophical-medical thought-experiment. He also emphasised the central position occupied by the problem in Berkeley's thought: the establishment of the heterogeneity of sight and touch was a challenge to the prevailing doctrine of extension, and that in turn was a challenge to the prevailing doctrine of matter and substance.[19]

Articles specifically devoted to the Molyneux problem have appeared in the *Journal of the History of Ideas*. Colin Turbayne in the course of an article on 'Berkeley and Molyneux on retinal images' discussed the divergence between Berkeley's theory of how we come to see bodies in space and that of writers on optics, including Molyneux. The latter accepted the Cartesian view that the act of seeing is an act of judgment, Berkeley denied this. Turbayne observed that it was Molyneux's problem that gave Berkeley the clue to his own explanation: a man born blind and made to see would not be able to see bodies in space until he had touched them while he looked. Berkeley denied 'the common error of the opticians that there is a necessary connection between colours and bodies in space'.[20] J. W. Davis in 'The Molyneux problem' stressed the conditional nature of Locke's negative response and suggested that he differed 'but by a hair's breadth' from Leibniz, whose answer had been positive. Davis distinguished between the broad empiricism of Locke, which linked judgment to sensation, and the 'narrowly conceived' empiricism of Berkeley. He called Diderot's view, that time was required to enable a formerly blind man to perceive shapes by sight, a rationalist opinion.[21] Désirée Park in 'Locke and Berkeley on the Molyneux problem' did not differentiate the responses of Locke and Molyneux but drew a sharp distinction between the positions of Locke and Berkeley. However, she thought that Locke, Molyneux, and Berkeley had all reached the same correct conclusion.[22] David Berman was the first (1974) to show that Francis Hutcheson had an interest in the Molyneux problem, a discovery made from an improbable source, the *European Magazine,* in which a letter that Hutcheson wrote from Dublin in 1727 was eventually published in 1788. In it Hutcheson made the categorical statement that Locke and Molyneux were both wrong. Although Hutcheson did not mention Berkeley in this connection Berman suggests that his answer to the problem was clearly a reply to Berkeley: a surprising answer, as Hutcheson has commonly been regarded as an empiricist, and an affirmative answer to Molyneux has been regarded as the hallmark of a rationalist.[23]

David Berman also took part in a controversy, conducted in *The Times Literary Supplement,* in which he advanced the view that Locke on his own principles should not have given a negative answer to Molyneux's question. Locke held that we get our ideas of figure from both sight and touch, and therefore should also have held that the formerly blind man would at once recognise by sight the globe whose shape he already knew by touch. Locke's position was quite different from that of Berkeley, who held that there was nothing in common between the sense of touch and the sense of sight and that it was the sense of touch that enabled us to recognise figures.[24] However, Locke did give a negative answer. Though his empiricism was less thorough-paced than Berkeley's, enough of it remained to separate him from the rationalists who gave an affirmative answer to the question. Locke's intermediate position has been described as realistic and rationalistic empiricism.

What started as a 'jocose problem' has proved to have implications that have continued to be of relevance for nearly three hundred years. The problem has divided one philosopher from another, and some individual philosophers, leaning now this way and now that, have made it difficult to decide to which answer their reasoning has really led them.

Appendix B

THE SOUTHAMPTON COLLECTION

SOUTHAMPTON is an unexpected place in which to find an important collection of Molyneux books and papers, and the reason
for their being there is peculiar. The inspector for the Historical
Manuscripts Commission in his report on Southampton archives
noted that they contained seven of what he called the Molyneux
books. He presumed that they had been deposited in the muniments
of Southampton by some town clerk who had acted as attorney for
a member of the Molyneux family.[1]

But the story is much more remarkable. The chief character in it
is a Swiss adventurer named Nathanael St André, who was alleged
to have been a dancing-master who was apprenticed to a surgeon
and who developed an enthusiasm for anatomy.[2] He came to
England and was appointed anatomist at the court of George I.
At court he came into contact with Samuel Molyneux (William's
son), who was private secretary to the prince of Wales, and with
Samuel's wife, Lady Elizabeth, née Capel, who was attached to the
household of the princess. St André got into serious trouble over
the affair of Mary Tofts, who claimed that she had been frightened
by a rabbit in the early stages of her pregnancy and that she was
convinced she would give birth to rabbits. The local apothecary
asked St André to come to Godalming to supervise the delivery of
the rabbits. St André, accompanied by Samuel Molyneux, arrived
to be told that the apothecary had already delivered fifteen rabbits.
St André himself then allegedly delivered the sixteenth and seventeenth rabbits, stripped of their skin. He was so ill-advised as to
publish an account of his achievement, to the truth of which Samuel
Molyneux, with uncharacteristic imprudence, gave a testimonial.
George I was suspicious and sent two doctors to inquire, who
reported that the alleged delivery of rabbits was fraudulent. Mary
Tofts was prosecuted and confessed that the affair was an imposture,
effected by the introduction of pieces of membrane into her body.
The story caused a general horror and rabbit-phobia. It was said
that the rent of warrens sank to nothing and that no one ventured
to eat rabbit.

Members of the medical profession subscribed to pay Hogarth

for a cartoon which he entitled 'Cunicularii, or the three wise men
of Godliman in consultation'. Of the figures 'the dancing-master or
preternatural anatomist' was St André; 'an occult philosopher
searching into the depths of things' appears to have been Samuel
Molyneux; the third was a doctor.[3] Pope satirised the affair with
verses bearing the title 'The discovery, or the squire turned ferret:
an excellent new ballad to the tune of High boys, up go we; Chevy
Chase; or what you please'. The following stanzas will serve as a
sample:

> At Godliman hard by the Bull
> A woman long thought barren
> Bears rabbits, Gad, so plentiful
> You'd take her for a warren.
>
> .   .   .   .
>
> But M-l-n-x, who heard this told
> (Right wary he and wise)
> Cried sagely, 'tis not safe I hold
> To trust to D-nt's eyes.[4]
>
> A vow to God he then did make
> He would himself go down,
> St A-dré too the scale to take
> Of that phenomenon.

In Pope's version St André is alleged to have brought a rabbit with
him, cut it in pieces, put it in Mary Toft's body, and then duly
delivered the fragments.[5]

When St André next appeared at court he got such a reception
that he never returned. However, he continued to practise as a
doctor and, after Samuel Molyneux, who was a member for Exeter,
had had a fit in the house of commons in 1728, St André was called
in to attend him. Samuel died and it was alleged that he had been
poisoned, a rumour stimulated by the news that Lady Elizabeth had
gone off that night with St André. She later married him, and in
consequence was dismissed from her post by the former princess,
now Queen Caroline. The St Andrés found London life uncongenial,
and eventually settled in Southampton. St André, who outlived his
wife by many years, died in 1776 at the age of 96. He had two
illegitimate sons, the children of a maidservant named Mary Pitt,
and left the greater part of his estate to them. The bequest included

a number of Molyneux books and papers, which were given in 1831
to Southampton corporation by St André's younger son, George
Frederick Pitt, with the object of encouraging the pursuit of literature
and general information. The books were, however, too specialised
for such a purpose, and for many years little was done to make the
Pitt collection available to the public. The collection now consists
of 761 printed books, of which about 500 were published before
William Molyneux's death and may be presumed to have formed
part of the library acquired or inherited by him. His name is in a
number of them, and much of the collection reflects his special
interests. Much of that library was sold after Samuel's death, the
books being listed in a still surviving sale catalogue.[6] Besides printed
books the Pitt collection contains a number of manuscripts, including William Molyneux's correspondence with Flamsteed, his survey
of the Castle Dillon estate, a manuscript copy of *Ogygia,* and letter-
books and accountbooks of Samuel Molyneux.[7]

NOTES

CHAPTER I

1. Unless otherwise stated, biographical information is in general taken from Capel Molyneux, *An account of the family and descendants of Sir Thomas Molyneux, Kt, chancellor of the exchequer in Ireland to Queen Elizabeth* (Evesham, 1820). Sir Capel, who was the grandson of William Molyneux's brother Thomas, compiled the work from family papers and included a long autobiographical letter from William to his brother. In fact, the first Thomas was not a knight. Specific references to Sir Capel's *Account* are normally confined to quotations. *D.N.B.* has articles on the first Thomas, on William and his brother Sir Thomas, and on William's son Samuel.

2. P.R.O.I., *Thirteenth report of the Deputy Keeper*, app. iv, p. 80 (fiant 3325).

3. *Liber munerum publicorum Hiberniae*, ii, 48, 108.

4. See pedigree (facing p. 16), based on material in Genealogical Office, Dublin.

5. Capel Molyneux, *Account*, p. 9.

6. P.R.O.I., Lodge MSS, List of members of King's Inns, Dublin, 1607-1770.

7. Thomas Carte, *Life of Ormonde*, i (1736), pp. 404-5.

8. H.M.C., *Ormonde MSS*, ii, 244; Robert Dunlop (ed.), *Ireland under the commonwealth* (Manchester, 1913), ii, 704.

9. Capel Molyneux, *Account*, p. 27.

10. *Cal. S.P. Ire., 1660-2*, p. 314.

11. Clifford Walton, *History of the British standing army, A.D. 1660–1700* (London, 1894), p. 724.

12. Capel Molyneux, *Account*, p. 24.

13. Armagh Public Library, MS. H. II. 20 (Title, interest, and purchase of Castle Dillon).

14. Ibid., MS. H. II. 19 (Title to land near Gormond's Gate).

15. B.L., MS. K Top. liii (9); on Phillips's map, see further *A new history of Ireland*, ed. T. W. Moody, F. X. Martin, F. J. Byrne (Oxford, 1976), iii, 472, 476.

16. Capel Molyneux, *Account*, p. 22.

17. See J. G. Simms, 'Dublin in 1685', *Irish Historical Studies*, xiv (1965), pp. 212-26.

18. William to Thomas Molyneux, 12 Apr. 1684: *Dublin University Magazine*, xviii (1841), p. 480.

CHAPTER II

1. Capel Molyneux, *Account*, p. 54.

2. G. D. Burtchaell and T. U. Sadleir, *Alumni Dublinenses* (Dublin, 1935), p. 480.

3. W. B. S. Taylor, *History of the university of Dublin* (Dublin, 1845), p. 265; facing p. 530 is an illustration of a fellow commoner's gown.

4. J. P. Mahaffy, *The plate in Trinity College, Dublin* (Dublin, 1918), p. 25.

5. Constantia Maxwell, *History of Trinity College, Dublin, 1591–1892* (Dublin, 1946), chapters i-iii.

6. B.L., Add. MS. 4223, f. 34v.

7. Capel Molyneux, *Account*, p. 60.

8. For Symner see T. C. Barnard, 'Myles Symner and the new learning in seventeenth-century Ireland', *Jn. Royal Soc. of Antiquaries of Ire.*, cii, part 2 (1972), pp. 129-42.

9. Capel Molyneux, *Account*, p. 55.

10. B.L., MS. K Top. liii (9).

11. Capel Molyneux, *Account*, p. 55.

12. Ibid., p. 56.

13. E. R. McC. Dix, 'The Crooke family; printers in Dublin in the seventeenth century', *Bibliographical Soc. of Ire., Short papers*, ii (1920), pp. 16-17.

14. Southampton archives, MS. D/M 4/22.

15. Ibid., MS. D/M 4/16. The translation was of the *Discorsi* and not, as stated in K. T. Hoppen, *The common scientist in the seventeenth century* (London, 1970), pp. 128-30, of the *Dialogues concerning the two chief world systems*. I am indebted to Mrs Corinna Salvadori Lonergan for the estimate of Molyneux's translation.

16. Capel Molyneux, *Account*, p. 25.

17. Flamsteed to Molyneux, 2 Sept. 1681; Molyneux to Flamsteed, 17 Sept. 1681 (Southampton, MS. D/M 1/1, which contains original letters from Flamstee to Molyneux and Molyneux's letter-book with drafts or summaries of his letters to Flamsteed). Some letters of Molyneux to Flamsteed are printed in *A general dictionary*, ed. J. P. Bernard and others, vii (London, 1738), pp. 602-14. The originals of these have not been preserved.

18. Molyneux to Flamsteed, 17 Sept. 1681, (*General dictionary*, vii, 603).

19. Molyneux to Flamsteed, 11 Apr. 1682.

20. Molyneux to Flamsteed, 18 Apr. 1682.

21. Thomas Birch, *History of the Royal Society*, iv (London, 1757), pp. 406, 421.

22. B.L., Add. MS. 4811, f. 174.

23. Ibid., ff. 5v-7.

24. Ibid., f. 174v; Royal Soc., early letters M. 1. 92.

25. Molyneux to Flamsteed, 22 Dec. 1685, 20 Feb. 1686.

26. R. W. T. Gunther, *Early science in Oxford*, iv (Oxford, 1912), p. 171; xiii (1939), p. 107; Royal Soc., early letters M. 1. 91; Molyneux to Halley, 1 Apr. 1686 (Birch, iv, 475-9).

27. Halley to Molyneux, 27 May 1686 (E. F. MacPike, *Corr. and papers of Edmond Halley* (Oxford, 1932), pp. 64-5); Molyneux to Halley, 19 June 1686 (Royal Soc., early letters M. 1. 96).

28. Halley to Molyneux, 27 Mar. 1686 (MacPike, *op. cit.*, pp. 57-60); Molyneux Halley, 8 Apr. 1686 (Royal Soc., early letters M. 1. 94).

29. B.L., Add. MS. 4811, ff. 178v-9.

30. Molyneux to Flamsteed, 3 Mar. 1683.

31. Molyneux to Flamsteed, 11 Aug. 1683; Flamsteed to Molyneux, 7 Sept. 1683, 29 Mar. 1684.

32. Molyneux to Flamsteed, 8 Apr., 7 Aug. 1684.

33. Flamsteed to Molyneux, 4 Nov. 1686; Molyneux to Flamsteed, 13 Nov. 1686.

34. *Phil. Trans.*, xvi (1686), pp. 192-3.

35. Flamsteed to Molyneux, 17 Jan. 1687.

36. Molyneux to Flamsteed, 1 Feb. 1687, (*General dictionary*, vii, 608).

37. Molyneux to Flamsteed, 24 Mar. 1687, (*General dictionary*, vii, 609).

38. Flamsteed to Molyneux, 15 Apr., 3 Aug. 1687; Molyneux to Flamsteed, 17 May 1687.

39. I am grateful to Professor J. W. de Courcy and Dr John de Courcy Ireland for information about tides.

40. Molyneux to Flamsteed, 17 Sept. 1681, 1 Aug., 7 Oct. 1682; *D. U. Mag.*, xviii, 180.
41. Molyneux to Flamsteed, 11 Aug. 1683; *D. U. Mag.*, xviii, 487.
42. There are two copies in the library of T.C.D. (L. nn. 15, OO. o. 28).
43. Gunther, *Early science*, xii, 180.
44. Royal Soc., early letters T. 46, classified papers I. 20.
45. *Phil. Trans.*, xvi, 3-21; Molyneux to Halley, 19 June, 20 July 1686 (Royal Soc., early letters M. 1. 96, 97); Tollet to Molyneux, 17 July, 21 Sept. 1686 (Royal Soc., early letters T. 48, 49).
46. Molyneux to Flamsteed, 17 May 1687; Molyneux to Halley, 7 July 1687 (Royal Soc. copy letter-book, ii (1), 103). Thomas Molyneux, who brought part of the *Principia* to Dublin, arrived there at the end of April 1687 (*D. U. Mag.* xviii, 608).
47. Flamsteed to Molyneux, 19 Dec. 1687; Molyneux to Flamsteed, 19 May 1688 (*General dictionary*, vii, 611). Francis Robarts became a fellow of the Royal Society in 1673 and was president of the Dublin Philosophical Society in 1693.
48. *Dioptrica nova*, p. 216.
49. Molyneux to Sloane, 4, 13 Nov. 1697 (Royal Soc., early letters M. 1. 99; B.L. Sloane MS. 4036, f. 367).

CHAPTER III

1. E. G. R. Taylor, 'The English atlas of Moses Pitt', *Geographical Magazine*, xcv (1940), pp. 292-9.
2. K. T. Hoppen, *The common scientist in the seventeenth century* (London, 1970), pp. 21, 200-01. Dr Hoppen's book is a detailed and comprehensive account of the Dublin Philosophical Society. This, and other chapters owe much to it and to the mass of material relating to the society that Dr Hoppen has assembled for a volume to be published by the Irish Manuscripts Commission.
3. T.C.D., MS. 888/1, ff. 46, 80.
4. Edited by James Hardiman and published for the Irish Archaeological Society in 1846. For O'Flaherty see *D.N.B.*
5. R.I.A., MS. 12. W. 22, f. 6.
6. T.C.D., MS. 883/1, pp. 336-7. The version of Piers's account published in Charles Vallancey (ed.), *Collectanea de rebus Hibernicis*, i (Dublin, 1770) does not include the second quotation.
7. *D. U. Mag.*, xviii, 472.
8. Molyneux to Halley, 7 July 1687 (Royal Soc., copy letter-book ii (1), 104).
9. See further *New history of Ireland*, iii, 447-8.
10. *D. U. Mag.*, xviii, 316, 472.
11. O'Flaherty to Molyneux, 15 Dec. 1696 (T.C.D., MS. 888/1, f. 124).
12. *D. U. Mag.*, xviii, 472.
13. Benignus Millett, in *New history of Ireland*, iii, 574.
14. Samuel Molyneux to O'Flaherty, 9 Apr. 1708 (H.M.C., *Eleventh report*, app. iii, p. 36; *Galway Arch. Soc. Journal*, xviii (1938-9), pp. 183-5).
15. 'Journey to Connaught in 1709', *Miscellany of Ir. Arch. Soc.*, i (1846), p. 171. The journey is there wrongly attributed to Thomas Molyneux.
16. *D. U. Mag.*, xviii, 472.
17. Gunther, *Early science*, xii, 132.
18. *D. U. Mag.*, xviii, 478.

19. *D. U. Mag.*, xviii, 481.
20. J. T. Gilbert, *History of Dublin*, ii (Dublin, 1859), pp. 171-3.
21. *D. U. Mag.*, xviii, 483.
22. B.L., Add. MS. 4811, f. 163.
23. *D. U. Mag.*, xviii, 484.
24. Royal Soc. minutes, 2 Dec. 1685; *Phil. Trans.*, xv (1685), pp. 1236-8.
25. Ibid., xiv (1684), pp. 552-4.
26. BL., Add. MS. 4811, ff. 61v, 168v; *Phil. Trans.*, xv, 1108-12.
27. *D. U. Mag.*, xviii, 319; *Phil. Trans.*, xv, 820; P. I. Manning and others, *Geology of Belfast and the Lagan Valley* (2nd edn., Belfast, 1970), pp. 103-04. I am grateful to Professor G. L. Herries Davies for information on this point.
28. Vallancey, *Collectanea*, i, 56.
29. T.C.D., MS. 888/1, ff. 80, 82.
30. *Phil. Trans.*, xv, 876-9; *Acta Eruditorum* (1686), pp. 300-02.
31. B.L., Add. MS. 4811, f. 167.
32. Royal Soc., early letters, M. 1. 85; illustrated in Gunther, *Early science*, xii, 208.
33. B.L., Add. MS. 4811, f. 179.
34. *Phil. Trans.*, xv, 1032-5; *Acta Eruditorum* (1686), pp. 388-91.
35. B.L., Add. MS. 4811, f. 174v.
36. Hoppen, *Common scientist*, pp. 143-4; Edmond Fitzmaurice, *Life of Petty* (London, 1895), pp. 266-8.
37. Birch, *Hist. of Royal Soc.*, iv, 352-3.
38. *Phil. Trans.*, xv, 1028-9.
39. B.L., Add. MS. 4811, f. 71v.
40. B.L., Add. MS. 4811, ff. 182-3; T.C.D., MS. 655, ff. 48v-49; Marsh's Library, MS. ZZ. 2. 3, p. 30. There are copies of the questionnaire in Yale University Library and in the Pitt collection in Southampton Public Library.
41. National Library of Wales, Peniarth MS. 427, ff. 450-1. I am grateful to Mr William O'Sullivan, Keeper of MSS., T.C.D., for the reference.
42. Molyneux to Lhuyd, 7 Feb. 1695 (Bodleian Library, MS. Ashmole 1816, f. 370).
43. T.C.D., MS. 889/1, ff. 69-73.
44. *Phil. Trans.*, xix (1697), pp. 625-31.
45. Owen Lloyd to Richard Waller, 13 June 1694 (Royal Soc., early letters L. 5. 128).
46. Molyneux to Hans Sloane, 4 Nov. 1697 (ibid., M. 1. 99).
47. Hoppen, *Common scientist*, pp. 190-97.

CHAPTER IV

1. Copies and summaries of William and Thomas Molyneux's letters are printed in articles published anonymously by Sir William Wilde in *D. U. Mag.*, xviii (1841); that the articles were by Wilde is shown by *R.I.A. Proceedings*, iii (1847), p. 165.
2. Ibid., p. 314.
3. Ibid., p. 320.
4. Ibid., p. 473.
5. Ibid., p. 477.
6. Ibid., p. 486.
7. Birch, *Hist. of Royal Soc.*, iv, 384-6.
8. *Phil. Trans.*, xv (1685), pp. 880-81.

9. E. Labrousse, *Inventaire critique de la corréspondance de Pierre Bayle* (Paris, 1961), no. 272. I am indebted to Dr Hoppen for the reference.

10. *D. U. Mag.*, xviii, 488.

11. *Nouvelles de la république des lettres*, ii (1684), pp. 579-81.

12. Labrousse, no. 339.

13. *Nouvelles*, iii (1685), pp. 46-9.

14. *D. U. Mag.*, xviii, 485.

15. *Phil. Trans.*, xvi (1685), pp. 88-93.

16. Locke to Thomas Molyneux, 22 Dec. 1684 (O.S.) (*Locke Corr.*, ed. E. S. de Beer, ii, 669).

17. Locke to William Molyneux, 20 Sept. 1692.

18. *D. U. Mag.*, xviii, 480.

19. *Liber munerum publicorum Hiberniae*, ii, 106.

20. *D. U. Mag.*, xviii, 480.

21. S. W. Singer (ed.), *Clarendon and Rochester correspondence* (London, 1828), ii, 87.

22. Capel Molyneux, *Account*, p. 63.

23. Quoted in E. MacLysaght, *Irish life in the seventeenth century* (2nd edn., Cork, 1950), p. 386.

24. John Cornforth, 'Dublin Castle', *Country Life*, 30 July 1970.

25. *D. U. Mag.*, xviii, 605.

26. *Dioptrica nova*, p. 224.

27. Ibid., p. 281; Gunther, *Early science*, xii, 80.

28. B.L., Add. MS. 4811, ff. 124v, 125.

29. *Dioptrica nova*, pp. 223-4.

30. Ibid., p. 215. Molyneux seems to have confused Borel with Giovanni Alfonso Borelli, the Italian physiologist and astronomer (1608-74), whose discussion of lenses he mentions. Articles on both Borel and Borelli are in *Biographie universelle*.

31. Flamsteed to Molyneux, 11 Sept. 1685.

32. Flamsteed to Molyneux, 23 Nov. 1686. (Coast; side of meat, *O.E.D.*, coast, no. 1c.)

33. Berkeley, *Works*, ed. A. A. Luce and T. E. Jessop, iv (London, 1951), pp. 56-7.

34. Flamsteed to Newton, 26 Sept. 1685 (*Corr. of Isaac Newton*, ed. H. W. Turnbull, ii (Cambridge, 1960), p. 423).

35. Molyneux to Flamsteed, 22 Dec. 1685, 20 Feb. 1686.

36. *D. U. Mag.*, xviii, 607.

37. Singer, *Clarendon corr.*, ii, 128.

38. B.L., Add. MS. 4811, f. 180.

39. Birch, *Hist. of Royal Soc.*, iv, 503; *Phil. Trans.*, xvi (1686), pp. 213-16.

40. *Acta Eruditorum* (1687), pp. 623-6; *Bibliothèque universelle* (1686), pp. 326-9.

41. *Dioptrica nova*, p. 246.

42. D. J. Price, 'The early instruments of Trinity College, Cambridge', *Annals of Science*, viii (1952), p. 3 (cited in Hoppen, *Common scient*, p. 256).

44. Molyneux to Aston, 14 Nov. 1685 (Royal Soc., early letters, M. 1. 93); Gale to Ashe, 27 Mar. 1686 (B.L., Add. MS. 4811, f. 117).

45. Molyneux to Flamsteed, 22 Dec. 1685; 20 Feb. 1686.

46. Ibid.; Halley to Molyneux, 27 Mar. 1686 (*Corr. and papers of Edmond Halley*, ed. E. F. MacPike, pp. 57-60).

47. Birch, *Hist. of Roy. Soc.*, iv, 490, 499.

48. Gunther, *Early science*, xii, 204.

49. Molyneux to Flamsteed, 17 May 1687; Flamsteed to Molyneux, 19 Dec. 1687.
50. Royal Soc. minutes, 20 Mar. 1689.
51. Molyneux to Flamsteed, 7 Sept. 1689, (*General dictionary*, vii, 611).
52. J. A. Downie, 'The commission of public accounts and the formation of the country party', *English Historical Review*, xci (1976), p. 43.
53. Capel Molyneux, *Account*, p. 72.
54. Armagh Public Library, MS. H. II. 20. His father died on 23 Jan. 1693 in his 77th year. The last years of his life had been tortured by illness: 'his body was opened and in his bladder was found two stones, one of them of the size of a hen's egg, the other of a walnut' (Capel Molyneux, *Account*, p. 76).

CHAPTER V

1. As distinct from catoptrics, which treats of the reflection of light from polished surfaces.
2. Molyneux to Flamsteed, 11 Apr. 1682.
3. Ibid. Descartes showed that the ratio was to the sines of the angles.
4. Published 1679 and attributed to Obadiah Walker.
5. Flamsteed to Molyneux, 29 May 1682.
6. Royal Soc., early letters, H. 3. 72.
7. Molyneux to Halley, 10 Mar. 1687 (Royal Soc., record book 7, pp. 77-86).
8. Molyneux to Flamsteed, 24 Mar. 1687.
9. *Phil. Trans.*, xvi, 323-9.
10. Berkeley, *An essay towards a new theory of vision* (Dublin, 1709), sections 67-78.
11. Among others by Hans Neuberger, *Introduction to physical meteorology* (State College, Penn., 1951), p. 154; Lloyd Kaufman and Irvin Roch, 'The moon illusion', *Scientific American*, 207 (1962), pp. 120-30; E. J. Furlong, 'The varying visual sizes of the moon', *Astronomy and Space*, ii (1972), pp. 215-17.
12. Royal Soc., copy letter-book 10, 43-51.
13. *Phil. Trans.*, xvi (1686), pp. 169-72; *Bibliothèque universelle* (1686), pp. 329-34; Flamsteed to Molyneux, 5 Jan. 1687.
14. Flamsteed to Molyneux, 23 Nov. 1686; Molyneux to Flamsteed, 11 Dec. 1686.
15. Molyneux to Flamsteed, 7 May 1690.
16. Flamsteed to Molyneux, 10 May 1690.
17. Molyneux to Flamsteed, 17 May 1690; *Dioptrica nova*, pp. 192-5, 198-9.
18. *Biographia Britannica*, v, 3128; Molyneux to Halley, 8 Oct. 1690 (Royal Soc., early letters, M. 1. 98).
19. Huygens, *Oeuvres complètes*, xiii (The Hague, 1916), p. 829.
20. Berkeley, *Theory of vision*, sections 88-120.
21. Ibid., section 90.
22. Berkeley, *Theory of vision ... vindicated* (1733), section 50. Berkeley's view is discussed in Colin Turbayne, 'Berkeley and Molyneux on retinal images', *Journal of the History of Ideas*, xvi (1955), pp. 345-55.
23. Barrow, *Lectiones opticae* (London, 1674), xviii, section 13; Huygens, *Oeuvres*, xiii, 830; Berkeley, *Theory of vision*, sections 39, 40. I am grateful to Professors T. D. Spearman, P. A. Wayman, and E. T. S. Walton for advice on this question.

24. *Dioptrica nova*, p. 294.
25. Capel Molyneux, *Account*, p. 76.
26. Samuel Molyneux to ——, 18 Feb. 1713 (Southampton MS. D/M 1/3, f. 101).
27. B.L., press-mark 537.K.17. Boyle had died on 30 Dec. 1691, but Molyneux seems not to have known this when he drew up his list of recipients.
28. *Acta Eruditorum*, Jan. 1693, pp. 1-5.
29. Huygens, *Oeuvres*, x, 260, 279.
30. Ibid., xiii, 826-34; Leibniz, *New essays concerning human understanding*, trans. A. G. Langley (New York, 1896), p. 484.
31. Transcribed by Molyneux in his annotated copy of *Dioptrica nova* (B.L., 537.K.17.)
32. Capel Molyneux, *Account*, p. 76.
33. Benjamin Tooke to Samuel Molyneux, 8 Feb. 1709 (Southampton, MS. D/M 1/2).
34. *General dictionary*, vii, 69.
35. *Biographia Britannica*, v, 3129.
36. Berkeley, *Philosophical commentaries*, ed. A. A. Luce (London, 1944), pp. 327-8n.

CHAPTER VI

1. Locke to Molyneux, 16 July 1692. The main authority for this chapter is the published correspondence of Locke and Molyneux (first published in *Some familiar letters between Mr Locke and several of his friends* (1708); the most recent edition is by E. S. de Beer, Oxford, 1976-).
2. Molyneux to Locke, 27 Aug. 1692.
3. Locke to Molyneux, 20 Sept. 1692; 26 Dec. 1692.
4. Molyneux to Locke, 22 Dec. 1692.
5. Ibid.
6. Thomas Molyneux to Locke, 20 Dec. 1692; Locke to Thomas Molyneux, 20 Jan. 1693; William Molyneux to Locke, 2 Mar. 1693.
7. Molyneux to Locke, 22 Dec. 1692; Locke to Molyneux, 20 Jan. 1693.
8. Molyneux to Locke, 2 Mar. 1693; Locke to Molyneux, 28 Mar. 1693.
9. Molyneux to Locke, 18 Apr. 1693.
10. Molyneux to Locke, 22 Dec. 1692; Locke to Molyneux, 20 Jan. 1693.
11. Locke to Molyneux, 15 July 1693; Molyneux to Locke, 12 Aug. 1693.
12. Locke to Molyneux, 23 Aug. 1693; Molyneux to Locke, 16 Sept. 1693.
13. Molyneux to Locke, 28 July 1694.
14. Locke to Molyneux, 20 Jan. 1693; Molyneux to Locke, 2 Mar. 1693.
15. Locke to Molyneux, 23 Aug. 1693; Molyneux to Locke, 16 Sept. 1693.
16. Molyneux to Locke, 23 Dec. 1693; Locke to Molyneux, 19 Jan. 1694.
17. Locke to Molyneux, 28 Mar. 1693; Molyneux to Locke, 18 Apr. 1693.
18. Molyneux to Locke, 2 Mar. 1693; Molyneux to authors of the *Bibliothèque universelle*, 7 July 1688 (*Locke Corr.*, ed. de Beer, iii, 482-3).
19. Molyneux to Locke, 28 July 1694.
20. Molyneux to Locke, 24 Dec. 1695; Locke to Molyneux, 30 Mar. 1696.
21. See Appendix A.
22. Molyneux to Locke, 28 July 1694; Locke to Molyneux, 3 Sept. 1694.
23. Locke to Molyneux, 8 Mar. 1695.
24. Molyneux to Locke, 15 Jan. 1695; Locke to Molyneux, 8 Mar. 1695.

25. Molyneux to Locke, 7 May 1695; Locke to Molyneux, 2 July 1695.

26. Molyneux to Locke, 24 Aug. 1695; Locke to Molyneux, 20 Nov. 1695. Burridge's *Historia nuperae rerum mutationis in Anglia* duly appeared under the Churchill imprint in the summer of 1697.

27. Locke to Molyneux, 2 July 1696; Molyneux to Locke, 19 Apr. 1698.

28. Molyneux to Locke, 27 Aug. 1692; Locke to Molyneux, 20 Sept. 1692.

29. Molyneux to Locke, 22 Dec. 1692; Locke, *Essay concerning human understanding,* bk iv, chap. xx, sec. 3, (chap. xxi in 2nd and subsequent editions).

30. Molyneux to Locke, 2 June 1694.

31. Molyneux to Locke, 14 Mar. 1696; Locke to Molyneux, 30 Mar. 1696.

32. Molyneux to Locke, 2 Mar. 1693.

33. Locke to Molyneux, 28 Mar. 1693; Molyneux to Locke, 18 Apr. 1693.

34. Molyneux to Locke, 12 Aug., 16 Sept. 1693; Locke to Molyneux, 23 Aug. 1693.

35. Locke, *Some thoughts concerning education,* para 106.

36. Molyneux to Locke, 12 Aug. 1693; Locke to Molyneux, 23 Aug. 1693.

37. Molyneux to Locke, 12 Aug. 1693.

38. Molyneux to Locke, 2 June, 28 July 1694; Locke to Molyneux, 28 June 1694.

39. Molyneux to Locke, 7 May, 24 Aug. 1695.

40. Locke to Molyneux, 3 May 1697; Molyneux to Locke, 27 May 1697; Locke to Molyneux, 10 Jan. 1698.

41. Locke to Molyneux, 2 July, 16 Nov. 1695.

42. Molyneux to Locke, 6 June 1696; Locke to Molyneux, 2 July 1696; Molyneux to Locke, 26 Sept. 1696.

43. Benjamin Furly to Locke, 9/19 Aug. 1693 (*Locke Corr.,* ed. de Beer, iv, 710-11). See also J. G. Simms, 'John Toland: a Donegal heretic', *Irish Historical Studies,* xvi (1969), pp. 304-20.

44. J. C. Biddle, 'Locke's critique of innate principles and Toland's deism', *Journal of the History of Ideas,* xxxvii (1976), 411-22.

45. Molyneux to Locke, 16 Mar., 6 Apr. 1697; Locke to Molyneux, 3 May 1697.

46. Molyneux to Locke, 27 May 1697; Locke to Molyneux, 15 June 1697.

47. Molyneux to Locke, 26 July 1697.

48. King to Molyneux, 26 Oct. 1697; Molyneux to Locke, 28 Oct. 1697; Locke to Molyneux, 10 Jan. 1698; King to archbishop of Canterbury, 28 Sept. 1708 (T.C.D., MS. 750/3, pp. 246-7; I am indebted to Miss Isolde Victory for this reference).

49. Locke to Molyneux, 28 Mar., 15 July 1693.

50. Locke to Molyneux, 23 Nov. 1694; Molyneux to Locke, 18 Dec. 1694; Locke to Molyneux, 8 Mar. 1695.

51. Locke to Molyneux, 26 Apr. 1695; Molyneux to Locke, 7 May 1695; Locke to Molyneux, 2 July 1695.

52. Molyneux to Locke, 24 Aug. 1695; Locke to Molyneux, 16 Nov. 1695.

53. Molyneux to Locke, 6 June 1696; Locke to Molyneux, 2 July, 2 Sept. 1696.

54. Molyneux to Locke, 6 Apr., 12 Sept. 1697; David Piper, *Catalogue of seventeenth-century portraits in the National Portrait Gallery* (London, 1963), p. 209.

CHAPTER VII

1. The Williamite government continued Molyneux as joint surveyor-general, disregarding Tyrconnell's order for his removal (see pp. 51-2, 57 above).
2. J. C. Beckett, 'The Irish parliament in the eighteenth century', *Proceedings of the Belfast Natural History and Philosophical Society*, 2nd series, iv (1955), pp. 17-37; J. L. McCracken, *The Irish parliament in the eighteenth century* (Dundalk, 1971).
3. T.C.D., MS. MUN/V/5/2, p. 294 (minutes of college board).
4. Edmund Curtis and R. B. McDowell (ed.), *Irish historical documents* (London, 1943), p. 141.
5. Capel Molyneux, *Account*, pp. 73-4; *Cal. S.P. dom., 1692-3*, p. 91.
6. Molyneux to Locke, 24 Aug. 1695.
7. T.C.D., MS. 1179 (9).
8. Molyneux to Locke, 24 Aug. 1695.
9. Locke to Molyneux, 20 Nov. 1695.
10. Bodleian Library, MS. Locke b. 3, ff. 68-9, 'Propositions sent to the lords justices'. The lords justices were the members of the council of regency that functioned during William's absences in Holland.
11. Molyneux to Locke, 24 Dec. 1695.
12. T.C.D., MS. 888/1, ff. 104-05; R. R. Steele (ed.), *Tudor and Stuart proclamations*, ii (Oxford, 1910), pp. 161, 177. I am grateful to Dr P. H. Kelly for drawing my attention to this paper and for help with Locke's writings on coinage.
13. *Commons' jn. (Ire.)*, ii, 2 (1796), p. lxxx.
14. Molyneux to Locke, 6 June 1696.
15. Internuncio Orazio Spada to Cardinal Spada, 1 Nov. 1697, *Collectanea Hibernica*, no. 4 (1961), p. 62.
16. J. G. Simms, 'The bishops' banishment act of 1697', *Irish Historical Studies*, xvii (1970), pp. 185-99; C. S. King, *A great archbishop* (London, 1908), pp. 88-90.
17. Molyneux to Locke, 3 Feb. 1697.
18. Locke to Molyneux, 22 Feb. 1697; John Freke and Edward Clarke to Locke, 6 Apr. 1697.
19. Molyneux to Locke, 15 May 1697, 16 Mar. 1698; J. G. Simms, *Williamite confiscation* (London, 1956), p. 87.
20. 18 Charles II, c. 18.
21. Locke to Molyneux, 12 Sept. 1696. The politics of textiles are examined by H. F. Kearney, 'The political background to English mercantilism, 1695-1700', *Economic History Review*, 2nd ser., xi (1959), pp. 484-96, and more recently by P. H. Kelly, 'The Irish woollen export prohibition act of 1699: Kearney revisited', *Irish Economic and Social History*, vii (1980), 22-44.
22. Molyneux to Locke, 26 Sept. 1696.
23. Molyneux to Locke, 4 Oct. 1697.
24. Locke to Molyneux, 10 Jan. 1698.
25. Molyneux to Locke, 15 Mar. 1698.
26. *Commons' jn.* (Eng.), xii, 7, 44.
27. H.M.C., *Portland MSS*, iv, 222.
28. William King to Sir Robert Southwell, 10 Jan. 1698 (B.L. Egerton MS. 917, ff. 151-3). For Toland's experiences in Ireland, see p. 88 above.
29. John Methuen to Lord Galway, 25 Jan. 1698 (B.L., Sunderland letter-book 3).
30. Methuen to Galway, 15 Jan. 1698 (ibid.).

31. Methuen to Galway, 18 Jan. 1698 (ibid.).
32. Methuen to Galway, 8, 22 Feb. 1698 (ibid.); Conrad Gill, *Rise of the Irish linen industry* (Oxford, 1925), pp. 16-28.
33. James Vernon to duke of Shrewsbury, 12 Feb. 1698 (*Letters illustrative of the reign of William III* (ed. G. P. R. James, London, 1841), ii, 9); *Commons' jn.* (Eng.), xii, 123; Methuen to Galway, 14 Apr. 1698 (B.L., Sunderland letter-book 3).
34. Methuen to Galway, 4 June 1698 (ibid.).
35. *Lords' jn.* (Eng.), xvi, 314-15 (9 June 1698); *Commons' jn.* (Eng.), xii, 338 (27 June 1698).
36. Ibid., xii, 339 (2 July 1698).

CHAPTER VIII

1. Curtis and McDowell, *Irish historical documents*, p. 74.
2. Patrick Darcy, *An argument delivered . . . by the express order of the House of Commons in the Parliament of Ireland, 9 Junii 1641* (Waterford, 1643; reprinted Dublin, 1764).
3. 16 Charles I, c. 33; Curtis and McDowell, *Irish historical documents*, p. 154.
4. T.C.D., MS. 890.
5. Curtis and McDowell, *Irish historical documents*, pp. 169-71.
6. See p. 100 above.
7. King to Sir Robert Southwell, 6 Jan. 1698 (B.L., Egerton MS. 917, ff. 151-2).
8. *Lord's jn.* (Eng.), xvi, 292 (24 May 1698).
9. Marsh's Library, MS. ZZ. 2. 5 (77).
10. *Case*, p. 2.
11. Ibid., preface.
12. Ibid., p. 27; for a detailed comparison of *Two treatises* with the *Case* see Locke, *Two treatises of government*, ed. Peter Laslett (Cambridge, 1960).
13. T.C.D., MS. 888/1.
14. *Case*, p. 29.
15. Ibid., p. 14.
16. Ibid., p. 20.
17. Ibid., pp. 26-7.
18. Ibid., p. 91.
19. Ibid., pp. 97-8.
20. Ibid., p. 99.
21. Ibid., p. 101.
22. King to Annesley, 16 Apr. 1698 (T.C.D., MS. 750/1, p. 211).
23. *Case*, p. 109.
24. Ibid., pp. 111-12.
25. Ibid., p. 148.
26. Ibid., p. 150.
27. Ibid., pp. 170-1.
28. Ibid., p. 174.
29. Afterword by Denis Donoghue in reissue of 1698 edition of the *Case* (Dublin, 1977: Cadenus Press).
30. T.C.D., MS. 890; the quotation is on p. 84. See further P. H. Kelly, 'The MS. of the printer's copy of William Molyneux's *Case of Ireland stated*', *Long Room*, xvi (1980), pp. 6-13.
31. King to Annesley, 16 Apr. 1698 (T.C.D., MS. 750/1, p. 211).

32. P. H. Kelly, 'Locke and Molyneux: the anatomy of a friendship', *Hermathena*, cxxvi (1979), p. 47.
33. Molyneux to Locke, 15 Mar. 1698. This suggests that at some earlier stage Locke had admitted to Molyneux his authorship of the *Two treatises*.
34. Molyneux to Locke, 19 Apr. 1698.
35. Locke to Edward Clarke, 30 May 1698; the letter does not name Molyneux, but the context makes it almost certain that the reference is to him.
36. Locke to Clarke, 25 Feb. 1698.
37. *Cal. S.P. dom., 1698*, pp. 261-2.
38. Methuen to Lord Galway, 3, 21 May 1698 (B.L., Blenheim papers, Sunderland letter-book 3).
39. *Cal. S.P. dom., 1698*, pp. 261-2; Methuen to Galway, 2 June 1698 (Sunderland letter-book 3).
40. *Commons' jn. (Eng.)*, xii, 324-6; Vernon to Shrewsbury, 28 June 1698 (*Letters illustrative*, ii, 115).
41. Ibid., pp. 337, 339.
42. Methuen to Galway, 26 May, 7 June 1698 (Sunderland letter-book 3).
43. King to bishop of Killaloe, 7 June 1698; King to Annesley, 25 June 1698 (T.C.D., MS. 750/1, pp. 241, 246).
44. Ezekiel Burridge, *A short view* (Dublin, 1708), preface.
45. King to Annesley, 16 July 1698 (T.C.D., MS. 750/1, p. 242).
46. Cary, *Vindication*, dedication.
47. Ibid., p. 127.
48. Atwood, *History and reasons*, pp. 16, 207.
49. John Harrison and Peter Laslett (ed.), *The library of John Locke* (2nd edn., Oxford, 1971), p. 110.
50. Leslie, *Considerations*, p. 7.
51. *Commons' jn. (Ire)*, ii 342; *Lords' jn. (Ire.)*, ii 8.
52. Swift, *Works*, ix (1969), pp. 1-12.
53. Curtis and McDowell, *Irish historical documents*, p. 186 (6 Geo 1, c. 65).
54. Swift, *Works*, x (1966), pp. 62-3.
55. Charles Lucas, *A tenth address* (Dublin, 1748), p. 114.
56. *Faulkner's Dublin Journal*, 3-7 Oct. 1749.
57. A. H. Smyth (ed.), *The writings of Benjamin Franklin*, v (N.Y., 1907), pp. 254-5; H. A. Cushing (ed.), *The writings of Samuel Adams*, ii (N.Y., 1906), pp. 254-64.
58. *Parliamentary register*, i (Dublin, 1782), p. 425.
59. *Dublin Evening Post*, 29 Sept. 1781.
60. Henry Grattan, *Speeches*, i (Dublin, 1822), p. 123.

CHAPTER IX

1. Locke to Molyneux, 6 Apr. 1698.
2. Molyneux to Locke, 19 Apr. 1698.
3. Molyneux to Locke, 15 Mar. 1698.
4. King to Annesley, 16 July 1698 (T.C.D., MS. 750/1, p. 242).
5. Locke to Molyneux, 9 July 1698.
6. Molyneux to Locke, 20 Sept. 1698.
7. P.R.O., CO 391/11 (Board of trade journal); I am grateful to Dr E. S. de Beer for the reference.
8. Molyneux to Locke, 20 Sept. 1698.

9. Locke to John Clovel, 26 July 1698.
10. Bodleian Library, MS. Locke f. 10.
11. Sylvester Brounower to Locke, 15 Nov. 1698.
12. Locke to Anthony Collins, 11 Sept. 1704.
13. *D. U. Mag.*, xviii, 751.
14. W. G. Strickland, *Dictionary of Irish artists*, i, 501.
15. King to Annesley, 10 Aug. 1698 (T.C.D., MS. 750/2, p. 17).
16. Molyneux to Locke, 20 Sept. 1698.
17. Locke to Molyneux, 29 Sept. 1698.
18. Ezekiel Burridge to Locke, 13 Oct. 1698, contains an account of Molyneux's death and of the four kidney stones found at his autopsy. Among his last words was a message for Locke.
19. Walter Harris, *The history of the writers of Ireland* (Dublin, 1764), pp. 259-60.
20. Locke to Thomas Molyneux, 27 Oct. 1698.
21. Thomas Molyneux to Locke, 26 Nov. 1698; Locke acknowledged receiving the money, 25 Jan. 1699.
22. Caroline Robbins, *The eighteenth-century commonwealthman* (Cambridge, Mass., 1959).
23. Capel Molyneux, *Account*, pp. 60, 64, 68.
24. Ibid., p. 65.
25. A recent account makes a very favourable assessment of his scientific achievement as investigator and organiser (*Dictionary of scientific biography*, vol. ix (New York, 1974), pp. 464-6).

APPENDIX A

1. See pp. 78-9 above.
2. Gottfried Leibniz, *Nouveaux essais sur l'entendement humain* (Amsterdam and Leipzig, 1765): English translation by A. G. Langley (New York, 1896), vol. ii, chap. 9, sec. 6.
3. London, 1702.
4. George Berkeley, *An essay towards a new theory of vision* (Dublin, 1709), sections 132-6.
5. *Tatler*, no. 55 (1709), pp. 23-6.
6. Benjamin Rand (ed.), *Berkeley and Percival* (Cambridge, 1914), p. 117.
7. Francis Hutcheson to William Mace, 6 Sept. 1727, first published in *European Magazine*, Sept. 1788, pp. 158-60, reproduced in David Berman 'Francis Hutcheson on Berkeley and the Molyneux problem' (*R.I.A. Proceedings*, lxxiv, sec. C (1974), pp. 259-65).
8. *Phil. Trans.*, xxxv (1728), pp. 447-50.
9. François Marie Arouet de Voltaire, *The elements of Newton's philosophy* (London, 1738), pp. 59-71.
10. R. S. Smith, *Complete system of optics* (Cambridge, 1738), i, 42-6; ii, 'Remarks', pp. 50-1.
11. Etienne de Condillac, *Essai sur l'origine des connaissances humaines* (Paris, 1746), part i, sect. 6.
12. Condillac, *Traité sur les sensations* (Paris, 1754), part iii, chapters 5, 6; English translation by Geraldine Carr (London, 1930), pp. 29, 171-80.
13. Denis Diderot, *Lettre sur les aveugles* (Paris, 1749).

14. Thomas Reid, *An inquiry into the human mind* (Edinburgh, 1764), in *Works*, ed. William Hamilton (Edinburgh, 1846), pp. 136-7.

15. Joseph Priestley, *History . . . of vision, light and colours* (London, 1772), pp. 720-24.

16. T. K. Abbott, *Sight and touch* (London, 1864), pp. 140-62; 'Fresh light on Molyneux's problem', *Mind*, n.s., xiii, no. 52 (1904), pp. 1-12; Berkeley, *Theory of vision*, sec. 133.

17. Ernst Cassirer, *The philosophy of the enlightenment* (Boston, 1951), pp. 109-10: translation of *Die Philosophie der Aufklärung* (Tübingen, 1932).

18. A. A. Luce, *Berkeley and Malebranche* (London, 1934), pp. 36-9.

19. H. M. Bracken, *Berkeley* (London, 1974), pp. 22, 29-30.

20. *Journal of the History of Ideas*, xvi (1955), pp. 339-55.

21. Ibid., xxi (1960), pp. 392-408.

22. Ibid., xxx (1969), pp. 253-60.

23. See note 7, above.

24. *Times Literary Supplement*, 21 June 1974.

APPENDIX B

1. H.M.C., *Eleventh report*, appendix iii, pp. 39-40.

2. For St André, see *D.N.B.*

3. *British Medical Journal* (1896), ii, 209-10; William Hogarth, *Works*, ed. John Nicholls and George Steevens (London, 1808), i, 464-92; *Gentleman's Magazine* (1842), i, 366.

4. Davenant, who brought the story to the court.

5. Alexander Pope, *Minor Poems*, ed. Norman Ault (London, 1954), pp. 259-64.

6. T.C.D., press-mark VV.i.45.

7. *Catalogue of the Pitt collection* (Southampton, 1964).

BIBLIOGRAPHY

I. MANUSCRIPT SOURCES

A. Ireland

1. Armagh Public Library
   MS. H. II. 19 (title to land near Ormond's Gate, Dublin)
   MS. H. II. 20 (title, interest, and purchase of Castle Dillon, Co. Armagh)
2. Marsh's Library, Dublin
   MS. Zz. 2. 3. (diary of Narcissus Marsh)
   MS. Zz. 2. 5. (77) (notes from the parliament rolls of Ireland by the lord bishop of Derry, the bishop of Clogher and Mr Molyneux)
3. Public Record Office of Ireland, Dublin
   Lodge MSS. (list of members of King's Inns, Dublin, 1607-1770)
4. Royal Irish Academy, Dublin
   MS. 12. W. 22 (Molyneux papers)
5. Trinity College, Dublin
   MS. MUN / V / 5 / 2 (College Register, ii (board minutes)
   MS. 622 (extracts from journals of Irish House of Commons, 1613-97)
   MS. 655 (members of Dublin Philosophical Society, 1693)
   MSS. 750/1-750/3 (letter-books of William King)
   MSS. 883, 888-9 (Molyneux papers)
   MS. 890 (MSS. of Domville's Disquisition and Molyneux's *Case of Ireland's being bound*)

B. Britain

1. National Library of Wales, Aberystwyth
   Peniarth MS. 427, ff. 450-1 (draft letter of Edward Lhuyd to ——, *c.* 1686)
2. British Library, London
   Add. MS. 4223 (short account of Molyneux's life)
   Add. MS. 4811 (minutes of Dublin Philosophical Society, 1684-93)
   Egerton MS. 917 (letters from Bishop King to Sir R. Southwell, Jan. 1698)

Sloane MS. 4036 (letter from William Molyneux to Hans Sloane, 13 Nov. 1697)

MS. K Top. liii (9) (map of Dublin, 1685)

Blenheim papers, Sunderland letter-book 3 (letters from John Methuen and Lord Somers to Lord Galway, 1697-8)

3. Public Record Office, Kew

MS. CO/391/9–391/11 (journals of the Board of Trade, 1696-9)

4. Royal Society, London

Classified papers, I. 20

Copy letter-book, ii (1)

Early letters, H. 3, 72; L. 5, 128; M. 1, 85, 91-99; T. 46, 48, 49

Minute books (1685)

Record book 7

5. Bodleian Library, Oxford

MS. Ashmole 1816 (letter from William Molyneux to Edward Lhuyd, 7 Feb. 1684/5)

MS. Locke b. 3 (papers relating to coinage)

6. Southampton Corporation Archives, Southampton

MS. D/M 1/1 (correspondence of William Molyneux and John Flamsteed, 1682-90)

MS. D/M 1/2 (letter-book of Samuel Molyneux, 1707-9)

MS. D/M 1/3 (letters of Samuel Molyneux, 1713)

MS. D/M 2/1 (survey of Castle Dillon estate, Co. Armagh)

MS. D/M 4/13 (translation by William Molyneux of Torricelli, *De motu gravium*)

MS. D/M 4/16 (translation by William Molyneux of Galileo, *Discorsi . . . intorno à due nuove scienze*)

MS. D/M 4/22 (summary by William Molyneux of John Donne, *Biathanatos*)

II. PRINTED SOURCES

Burtchaell, G. D., and Sadleir, T. U., (ed.), *Alumni Dublinenses* . . . 2nd edn. Dublin, 1935.

Calendar of state papers, domestic series, 1692-1698. 1900-33.

Calendar of state papers, Ireland, 1660-62. 1905.

Collectanea Hibernica, no. 4 (1961).

Courthope, James, 'Committee minutebook of House of Commons [England], 1697-9': *Camden Miscellany,* vol. xx (1953), pt 2.

Curtis, Edmund, and McDowell, R. B., (ed.), *Irish historical documents.* 1943.

Dunlop, Robert, (ed.), *Ireland under the Commonwealth. Being a selection of documents relating to the government of Ireland from 1651 to 1659.* 2 vols. Manchester, 1913.

Harrison, John, and Laslett, Peter, (ed.), *The Library of John Locke.* 2nd edn. Oxford, 1971.

Historical Manuscripts Commission,
   Eleventh report, appendix iii, Southampton Corporation manuscripts, (Molyneux papers). 1887.
   House of Lords Manuscripts, n. s., vol. iii, (1697-9). 1905.
   Ormonde Manuscripts, vol. ii. 1899.
   Portland Manuscripts, vol. iv. 1897.

Journals of the House of Commons [England], vol. xii. 1742.

Journals of the House of Commons of the kingdom of Ireland, vols. i, ii. Dublin, 1796.

Journals of the House of Lords [England], vol. xvi. [n.d.]

Journals of the House of Lords [Ireland], vols. i, ii. Dublin, 1779, 1780.

Labrousse, Elizabeth, (ed.), *Inventaire critique de la correspondance de Pierre Bayle.* Paris, 1961.

Liber munerum publicorum Hiberniae, ab an. 1152 usque ad 1827, ed. Rowley Lascelles. 2 vols. 1824, 1852.

Locke, John, *The correspondence of John Locke,* ed. E. S. de Beer. 8 vols. Oxford, 1976—.

MacPike, E. F., (ed.), *The correspondence and papers of Edmond Halley.* Oxford, 1932.

Modus tenendi parliamenta in Hibernia, ed. Anthony Dopping. Dublin, 1692.

Molyneux, Samuel, (1690-1728), *A catalogue of the library of the Honble. Samuel Molyneux, deceas'd . . . Consisting of many valuable and rare books in several languages . . . with several curious manuscripts, and all his mathematical, optical, and mechanical instruments.* 1730.

Molyneux, Samuel (1690-1728), 'Journey to Connaught—April, 1709', ed. Aquila Smith, *Miscellany of the Irish Archaeological Society,* vol. i (1846), 161-78.

Newton, Isaac, *The correspondence of Isaac Newton,* ed. H. W. Turnbull and others, vols. i-iv. Cambridge, 1959-67.

O'Flaherty, Roderick, 'A letter from Roderick O'Flaherty to William Molyneux, 29 Jan. 1697', ed. M. O'Duígeannáin, *Journal of the Galway Archaeological and Historical Society,* vol. xviii (1938-9), 183-5.

O'Roddy, Thady, 'Autograph letter of Thady O'Roddy', ed. J. H. Todd, *Miscellany of the Irish Archaeological Society,* vol. i (1846), 112-25.

The parliamentary register: or, a history of the proceedings and debates of the House of Commons of Ireland . . ., vol. i. Dublin, 1782.

Public Record Office of Ireland, *Thirteenth report of the deputy keeper,* appendix iv, (continuation of Fiants, Elizabeth). 1881.

Rand, Benjamin, (ed.), *Berkeley and Percival: the correspondence of George Berkeley* . . . *and Sir John Percival, afterwards earl of Egmont.* Cambridge, 1914.

Singer, S. W., (ed.), *The correspondence of Henry Hyde, earl of Clarendon and of his brother, Laurence Hyde, earl of Rochester* . . . 2 vols. 1828.

Southampton Public Library, Southampton, *Catalogue of the Pitt collection.* Southampton, 1964.

The statutes at large, . . . *from Magna Charta to the end of the session of parliament, March 14, 1704.* 4 vols. 1706.

The statutes at large passed in the parliaments held in Ireland . . . *1310-1698,* vols. i-iii. Dublin, 1786.

Steele, R. R., (ed.), *Bibliotheca Lindesiana* (vols. v, vi): *a bibliography of royal proclamations of the Tudor and Stuart sovereigns* . . ., *1484-1714.* 2 vols. Oxford, 1910.

Vallancey, Charles, (ed.), *Collectanea de rebus Hibernicis,* vol. i. Dublin, 1770.

Vernon, James, *Letters illustrative of the reign of William III, from 1696 to 1708, addressed to the duke of Shrewsbury* . . . *by J. Vernon, Esq., Secretary of State,* ed. G. P. R. James. 3 vols. 1841.

III. CONTEMPORARY BOOKS AND PAMPHLETS TO 1728
(death of Samuel Molyneux)

Acta Eruditorum. Leipzig, 1686-93.

Anderson, Robert, *The genuine use and effects of the gun demonstrated* . . . 1674.

Atwood, William, *The history, and reasons, of the dependency of Ireland upon the imperial crown of the kingdom of England, rectifying Mr Molineux's state of the case of Ireland's being bound by acts of parliament in England.* 1698.

Barrow, Isaac, *Lectiones XVIII, Cantabrigiae in scholis publicis habitae; in quibus opticorum phaenomenōn genuinae rationes investigantur, ac exponuntur.* 1674.

Berkeley, George, *The analyst; or, a discourse addressed to an infidel mathematician.* 1734.

Berkeley, George, *An essay towards a new theory of vision*. Dublin, 1709.

Berkeley, George, *Philosophical commentaries, generally called the Commonplace Book*, ed. A. A. Luce. 1944.

Berkeley, George, *The theory of vision, or visual language; shewing the immediate presence and providence of a deity vindicated, and explained*. 1733.

Berkeley, George, *Works*, ed. A. A. Luce and T. E. Jessop, vols. i, iv. 1948-51.

Bibliothèque universelle et historique, ed. Jean Le Clerc. Amsterdam, 1686-8.

Boate, Gerard, *Irelands naturall history*. 1652.

F. B. [Sir Francis Brewster], *An answer to a letter from a gentleman in the country, to a member of the House of Commons: on the votes of the 14th inst. relating to the trade of Ireland*. Dublin, 1698.

Browne, Peter, *A letter in answer to a book entitled Christianity not mysterious* . . . Dublin, 1697.

Burridge, Ezekiel, *Historia nuperae rerum mutationis in Anglia*. 1697.

Burridge, Ezekiel, *A short view of the present state of Ireland* . . . *written in 1700*. 1708.

Cary, John, *A discourse concerning the trade of Ireland and Scotland, as they stand in competition with the trade of England*. 1696.

Cary, John, *An essay on the state of England, in relation to its trade, its poor, and its taxes for carrying on the present war against France*. Bristol, 1695.

Cary, John, *A vindication of the parliament of England, in answer to a book written by William Molyneux of Dublin, Esq., intituled, The case of Ireland's being bound by acts of parliament in England, stated*. 1698.

[Clement, Simon], *An answer to Mr Molyneux his case of Ireland's being bound by acts of Parliament in England, stated, and his dangerous notion of Ireland's being under no subordination to the parliamentary authority of England refuted*. 1698.

[Cox, Sir Richard], *Some thoughts on the bill depending before the right honourable the House of Lords for prohibiting the exportation of the woollen manufactures of Ireland into foreign parts*. 1698.

Darcy, Patrick, *An argument delivered by Patricke Darcey, esquire; by the express order of the House of Commons in the Parliament of Ireland, 9 Junii 1641*. Waterford, 1641; reprinted Dublin, 1764.

Descartes, René, *Meditationes de prima philosophia* . . . Paris, 1641.

Donne, John, *Biathanatos: a declaration of that paradox or thesis that self-homicide is not so naturally sin, that it may never be otherwise.* 1644.

Edwards, John, *Socinianism unmask'd. A discourse shewing the unreasonableness of a late writer* [John Locke]'s *opinion concerning the necessity of only one article of Christian faith* . . . 1696.

Edwards, John, *The Socinian creed. Or a brief account of the professed tenets & doctrines of the foreigne and English Socinians* . . . *with proper antidotes against them.* 1697.

Enquiries to be propounded to the most ingenious of each county of Ireland. Dublin, 1693.

Fontenelle, Bernard de, *Entretiens sur la pluralité des mondes.* Paris, 1686; trans. by Sir William Domville (the younger) as *A discourse of the plurality of worlds,* Dublin, 1687.

Galilei, Galileo, *Dialogi . . . dove nei congressi di quattro giornate si discorre sopra i due massimi sistemi del mondo Tolemaico e Copernicano* . . . Florence, 1632.

Galilei, Galileo, *Discorsi e demostrazioni mathematichè intorno à due nuove scienze* . . . Leyden, 1638.

Hevelius, Joannes, *Annus climactericus; sive, rerum Uranicorum observationum annus quadragesimus nonus* . . . 1685.

Hevelius, Joannes, *Machina coelestis, pars prior . . . pars posterior* . . . Danzig, 1673-9.

Hooke, Robert, *Animadversions on the first part of the Machina coelestis.* 1674.

Huygens, Christiaan, *Astroscopia compendiaria tubi optici molimine liberata.* The Hague, 1684.

Huygens, Christiaan, *Horologium.* The Hague, 1658.

Huygens, Christiaan, *Oeuvres complètes de Christiaan Huygens,* vols. x, xiii. The Hague, 1905, 1916.

Huygens, Christiaan, *Systema Saturnium; sive, de causis mirandorum Saturni phenomenon, et comite ejus planeta novo.* The Hague, 1659.

Huygens, Christiaan, *Traité de la lumière* . . . Leyden, 1690.

Kepler, Iohannes, *Dioptrice, seu demonstratio eorum quae visui et visibilibus propter conspicilla nam ita pridem inventa sunt.* Augustae Vindelicorum, 1611.

Lee, Henry, *Anti-scepticism; or, notes upon each chapter of Mr. Lock's Essay concerning humane understanding.* 1702.

[Leslie, Charles], *Considerations of importance to Ireland: in a letter to a member of parliament there upon occasion of Mr Molyneux's book, intituled The case of Ireland's being bound by acts of parliament in England, stated.* Sine loco, 1698.

Locke, John, *An essay concerning human understanding*, 1690; 2nd edn., 1694; 3rd edn., 1695; 4th edn., 1700; definitive edn., ed. P. H. Nidditich, Oxford, 1975; *De intellectu humano editio quarta, aucta et emendata et nunc primum Latine reddita*, trans. Ezekiel Burridge, 1701; *Essai philosophique concernant l'entendement humain*, trans. Pierre Coste, Amsterdam, 1700.

Locke, John, *The reasonableness of Christianity, as delivered in the scriptures.* 1695.

Locke, John, *Further considerations concerning raising the value of money.* 1695.

Locke, John, *Several papers relating to money, interest and trade, &c. Writ upon several occasions, and published at different times.* 1696.

Locke, John, *Short observations on a printed paper, intituled, For encouraging the coining silver money in England, and after for keeping it here.* 1695.

Locke, John, *Some considerations of the consequences of the lowering of interest, and raising the value of money. In a letter to a member of parliament.* 1692; 2nd edn., 1696.

Locke, John, *Posthumous works.* 1706.

Locke, John, *Some familiar letters between Mr Locke and several of his friends.* 1708.

Locke, John, *Some thoughts concerning education.* 1693; 2nd edn., 1693; 3rd edn., 1695; 4th edn., 1699; definitive edn., ed. J. L. Axtell, Cambridge, 1968; *De l'éducation des enfants*, trans. P[ierre] C[oste], Amsterdam, 1695.

Locke, John, *Two treatises of government.* 1690; ed. P. Laslett, Cambridge, 1960.

Locke, John, *A letter to the right rev. Edward lord bishop of Worcester, concerning some passages relating to Mr Locke's Essay . . . in a late discourse of his lordship's in vindication of the Trinity.* 1697.

Locke, John, *Mr. Locke's reply to the lord bishop of Worcester's answer to his letter, concerning some passages . . . in vindication of the Trinity.* 1697.

Molyneux, Samuel, (1616-93), *Practical problems concerning the doctrine of projects, design'd for great artillery and mortarpieces.* [Dublin, 168?].

Molyneux, William, *Dioptrica nova: a treatise of dioptricks in two parts.* 1692.

Molyneux, William, *The case of Ireland's being bound by acts of parliament in England, stated.* Dublin, 1698. Reprinted with introduction by J. G. Simms and afterword by Denis Donoghue. Cadenus Press, Dublin, 1977. (refs. to original 1698 edn.).

Molyneux, William, *Sciothericum telescopicum: or, a new contrivance of adapting a telescope to an horizontal dial for observing the moment of time by day or night . . . With proper tables requisite thereto.* Dublin, 1686.

Molyneux, William, *Six metaphysical meditations wherein it is proved that there is a God,* trans. from the Latin of Descartes, with an introduction. 1680.

Newton, Isaac, *Opticks, or a treatise of the reflections, refractions & colours of light.* 1704.

Newton, Isaac, *Philosophiae naturalis principia mathematica.* 1687.

Nouvelles de la république des lettres, ed. Pierre Bayle, Amsterdam, vols. ii, iii, (1685-6).

O'Flaherty, Roderick, *A chorographical description of West or h-Iar Connaught written A.D. 1684,* ed. James Hardiman. Dublin, 1846.

O'Flaherty, Roderick, *Ogygia, seu rerum Hibernicarum chronologia* . . . 1685.

Petty, William, *Hiberniae delineatio, quoad hactenus licuit, perfectissima studio Guiliemi Petty, equitis aurati.* 1685.

The Philosophical Transactions of the Royal Society, vols. xiv-xix, xxxv, (1685-97, 1728).

Pitt, Moses, *The English atlas.* 4 vols. 1680-2.

Plot, Robert, *The natural history of Staffordshire.* Oxford, 1686.

Stillingfleet, Edward, bishop of Worcester, *A discourse in vindication of the doctrine of the Trinity.* 1697.

Synge, Edward, *A gentleman's religion.* 1697.

The Tatler, ed. Richard Steele, no. 55 (1709).

Toland, John, *Christianity not mysterious.* 1696.

[Toland, John: attributed], *A letter from a gentleman in the country to a member of the House of Commons in reference to the votes of the 14th instant.* 1697.

W[alker], O[badiah], *Propositions concerning optic-glasses.* Oxford, 1679.

IV. LATER WORKS

Abbott, T. K., 'Fresh light on Molyneux's problem', *Mind,* n.s., xiii (1904), 1-12.

Abbott, T. K., *Sight and touch: an attempt to disprove the received or Berkeleian theory of vision.* 1864.

...s, J. G., 'The bishops' banishment act of 1697', *Irish Historical Studies*, xvii (1970), 185-99.

...s, J. G., *Colonial Nationalism, 1698-1776*. Cork, 1976.

...s, J. G., 'Dublin in 1685', *Irish Historical Studies*, xiv (1965), ...12-26.

...s, J. G., *Jacobite Ireland, 1685-91*. 1969.

...s, J. G., 'John Toland (1670-1722), a Donegal heretic', *Irish Historical Studies*, xvi (1969), 304-20.

...s, J. G., *The Williamite confiscation in Ireland, 1690-1703*. ...956.

..., R. S., *A complete system of optics, in four books*. 2 vols. ...ambridge, 1738.

...land, W. G., *A dictionary of Irish artists*. 2 vols. 1913.

..., Jonathan, *The works of Jonathan Swift*, ed. Herbert Davis, ...ols. ix-x. Oxford, 1968, 1966.

...r, E. G. R., 'The English atlas of Moses Pitt', *Geographical Magazine*, xcv (1940), 292-9.

...r, W. B. S., *The history of the University of Dublin*. Dublin, ...845.

...ayne, Colin, 'Berkeley and Molyneux on retinal images', *Journal of the History of Ideas*, xvi (1955), 345-54.

...ire, F. M. A. de, *Eleméns de la philosophie de Newton, mis à ...a portée de tout le monde*, Amsterdam, 1738; trans. as *The ...elements of Newton's philosophy*, 1738.

...on, Clifford, *A history of the British standing army, A.D. 1660 ...o 1700*. 1894.

...e, Sir William], 'Gallery of illustrious Irishmen, no. XIII: Sir ...Thomas Molyneux, bart., M.D., F.R.S.', *Dublin University Magazine*, xviii (1841), 305-27, 470-90, 604-19, 744-64. ...(Prints numerous extracts from correspondence &c.).

The writings of Samuel Adams, ed. H. A. Cushing, vol. ii, New York, 1906.

Barnard, T. C., 'Myles Symner and the new learning in seventeenth-century Ireland', *Journal of the Royal Society of Antiquaries of Ireland,* cii, pt. 2 (1972), 129-42.

Beckett, J. C., 'The Irish parliament in the eighteenth century', *Proceedings of the Belfast Natural History and Philosophical Society,* 2nd ser., iv (1955), 17-37.

Berman, David, 'Francis Hutcheson on Berkeley and the Molyneux problem', *Proceedings of the Royal Irish Academy,* lxxiv, sec. C. (1974), 259-65.

Berman, David, Letter on the Molyneux problem, *Times Literary Supplement,* 21 June 1974.

Biddle, J. C., 'Locke's critique of innate principles and Toland's deism', *Journal of the History of Ideas,* xxxvii (1976), 411-22.

Biographia Britannica: or, the lives of the most eminent persons who have flourished in Great Britain and Ireland, from the earliest ages down to the present time . . . 6 vols. (in 7). 1747-66.

Biographie universelle . . . 83 vols. Paris, 1811-53.

Birch, Thomas, *The history of the Royal Society of London.* 4 vols. 1756-7.

Bracken, H. M., *Berkeley.* 1974.

Carte, Thomas, *A history of the life of James Duke of Ormonde . . . wherein is contained an account of the most remarkable affairs of his time . . .* 3 vols. 1735-6.

Cassirer, Ernst, *Die philosophie der aufklärung,* Tubingen, 1932; trans. as *The philosophy of the enlightenment,* F.C.A. Koelln and J. P. Pettegrove. Boston, 1951.

Condillac, Etienne de, *Essai sur l'origine des connaissances humaines.* Paris, 1746.

Condillac, Etienne de, *Traité sur les sensations.* Paris, 1754; trans. Geraldine Carr. 1930.

Cornforth, John, 'Dublin castle', *Country Life,* 30 July 1970.

Davis, J. W., 'The Molyneux problem', *Journal of the History of Ideas,* xxi (1960), 392-408.

The Dictionary of national biography, ed. Leslie Stephen and Sidney Lee. 66 vols. 1885-1901.

The Dictionary of scientific biography, ed. C. C. Gillispie. 15 vols. New York, 1970-8.

Diderot, Denis, *Lettre sur les aveugles, a l'usage de ceux qui voient.* Paris, 1749.

Dix, E. R. McC., 'The Crooke family; printers in Dublin in the seventeenth century', *Bibliographical Society of Ireland, Short Papers,* ii (1920), 16-7.

Downie, J. A., 'The commission of public accounts and the formation of the country party', *English Historical Review,* xci (1976), 33-51.

Dublin Evening Post, 1781.

Dublin University Magazine, vol. xviii (1841) (see under [Wilde, Sir W.]).

European Magazine, 1788.

Faulkner's Dublin Journal, 1749.

Fitzmaurice, Lord Edmond, *The life of Sir William Petty.* 1895.

The writings of Benjamin Franklin, ed. A. H. Smyth, vol. v, New York, 1907.

Furlong, E. J., 'The varying visual sizes of the moon', *Astronomy and Space,* ii (1972), 215-7.

A general dictionary, historical and critical; in which a new and accurate translation of that of . . . Mr Bayle is included, ed. J. P. Bernard and others. 10 vols. 1734-41.

Gentleman's Magazine, 1842.

Gill, Conrad, *The rise of the Irish linen industry.* Oxford, 1925.

Grattan, Henry, *His speeches in the Irish and imperial parliament,* ed. by his son. 4 vols. Dublin, 1822.

Gunther, R. W. T., *Early science in Oxford,* vols. iv, xii, xiii. Oxford, 1912, 1925, 1939.

Gilbert, J. T., *A history of the city of Dublin.* 3 vols. 1854-9.

Harris, Walter, *The history of the writers of Ireland.* Dublin, 1764.

Hogarth, William, *The genuine works of William Hogarth, illustrated . . .,* ed. John Nicholls and George Steevens, vol. i, 1808.

Hoppen, K. T., *The common scientist in the seventeenth century: a study of the Dublin Philosophical Society, 1683-1708.* 1970.

Kaufman, Lloyd, and Roch, Irvin, 'The moon illusion', *Scientific American,* 207 (1962), 120-30.

Kearney, H. F., 'The political background to English mercantilism, 1695-1700', *Economic History Review,* 2nd ser., xi (1959), 484-96.

Kelly, Patrick, 'Locke and Molyneux: the anatomy of a friendship', *Hermathena,* cxxvi (1979), 38-54.

Kelly, Patrick, 'The MS. of the printer's copy of William Molyneux's *Case of Ireland stated', Long Room,* xvi (1980), 6-13.

Kelly, Patrick, 'The Irish woollen export prohibition act of 1699: Kearney revisited', *Irish Economic and Social History,* vii (1980), 22-44.

King, C. S., *A great archbishop of Dublin, William King, D.D., 1650-1729.* 1908.

Leibniz, Gottfried, *Nouveaux essais sur Oeuvres philosophiques de feu M. L* Leipzig, 1765; trans. A. G. Langley.

Lucas, Charles, *A tenth address to the free of the city of Dublin.* Dublin, 1748.

Luce, A. A., *Berkeley and Malebranche.* 19

McCracken, J. L., *The Irish parliament i* Dundalk, 1971.

McLysaght, Edward, *Irish life in the se Cromwell.* 2nd edn. Cork, 1950.

Mahaffy, J. P., *The plate in Trinity College,*

Manning, P. I., and others, *The geology c valley.* 2nd edn. Belfast, 1970.

Maxwell, Constantia, *A history of Trinity 1892.* Dublin, 1946.

Molyneux, Sir Capel, Bt., *An account of th of Sir Thomas Molyneux, Kt., Chance Ireland to Queen Elizabeth.* Privately pr

Molyneux, Sir Capel, Bt., (ed.), *Anecdotes of patriot and philosopher Wm. Molyneux Ireland: Published from a manuscript wri* printed, Dublin, 1803.

Moody, T. W., Martin, F. X., and Byrne, F *of Ireland,* vol. iii: 'Early Modern Irel

Morgan, M. J., *Molyneux's question: vision, of perception.* Cambridge, 1977.

Neuberger, Hans, *Introduction to physical me* Penn., 1951.

Park, Désirée, 'Locke and Berkeley on th *Journal of the History of Ideas,* xxx (196

Piper, David, (ed.), *Catalogue of seventeenth- National Portrait Gallery.* 1963.

Pope, Alexander, *Minor Poems,* ed. Norman

Price, D. J., 'The early instruments of Trinit *Annals of Science,* viii (1952), 1-12.

Priestley, Joseph, *The history and present sta to vision, light and colours.* 1772.

Reid, Thomas, *An inquiry into the human min The works of Thomas Reid, D.D.: now* Sir William Hamilton, Bt. Edinburgh, 1

Robbins, Caroline, *The eighteenth-century cor* bridge, Mass., 1959.

Saunderson, Nicholas, *The elements of algebr* bridge, 1740.

Simm

Simm
Simm

Simm
Simm

Simn

Smith

Stricl
Swift

Tayle

Tayle

Turb

Volt

Walt

[Wil

INDEX

(WM *or* Molyneux *denotes* William Molyneux *the subject of the book. Members of the Molyneux family bearing the same christian name are differentiated by superscript numberals which permit identification under Molyneux in the index, e.g.* Samuel Molyneux³ *refers to* Samuel Molyneux, 1689-1728.)

The writings of Samuel Adams, ed. H. A. Cushing, vol. ii, New York, 1906.

Barnard, T. C., 'Myles Symner and the new learning in seventeenth-century Ireland', *Journal of the Royal Society of Antiquaries of Ireland,* cii, pt. 2 (1972), 129-42.

Beckett, J. C., 'The Irish parliament in the eighteenth century', *Proceedings of the Belfast Natural History and Philosophical Society,* 2nd ser., iv (1955), 17-37.

Berman, David, 'Francis Hutcheson on Berkeley and the Molyneux problem', *Proceedings of the Royal Irish Academy,* lxxiv, sec. C. (1974), 259-65.

Berman, David, Letter on the Molyneux problem, *Times Literary Supplement,* 21 June 1974.

Biddle, J. C., 'Locke's critique of innate principles and Toland's deism', *Journal of the History of Ideas,* xxxvii (1976), 411-22.

Biographia Britannica: or, the lives of the most eminent persons who have flourished in Great Britain and Ireland, from the earliest ages down to the present time . . . 6 vols. (in 7). 1747-66.

Biographie universelle . . . 83 vols. Paris, 1811-53.

Birch, Thomas, *The history of the Royal Society of London.* 4 vols. 1756-7.

Bracken, H. M., *Berkeley.* 1974.

Carte, Thomas, *A history of the life of James Duke of Ormonde . . . wherein is contained an account of the most remarkable affairs of his time . . .* 3 vols. 1735-6.

Cassirer, Ernst, *Die philosophie der aufklärung,* Tubingen, 1932; trans. as *The philosophy of the enlightenment,* F.C.A. Koelln and J. P. Pettegrove. Boston, 1951.

Condillac, Etienne de, *Essai sur l'origine des connaissances humaines.* Paris, 1746.

Condillac, Etienne de, *Traité sur les sensations.* Paris, 1754; trans. Geraldine Carr. 1930.

Cornforth, John, 'Dublin castle', *Country Life,* 30 July 1970.

Davis, J. W., 'The Molyneux problem', *Journal of the History of Ideas,* xxi (1960), 392-408.

The Dictionary of national biography, ed. Leslie Stephen and Sidney Lee. 66 vols. 1885-1901.

The Dictionary of scientific biography, ed. C. C. Gillispie. 15 vols. New York, 1970-8.

Diderot, Denis, *Lettre sur les aveugles, a l'usage de ceux qui voient.* Paris, 1749.

Dix, E. R. McC., 'The Crooke family; printers in Dublin in the seventeenth century', *Bibliographical Society of Ireland, Short Papers,* ii (1920), 16-7.

Downie, J. A., 'The commission of public accounts and the formation of the country party', *English Historical Review,* xci (1976), 33-51.

Dublin Evening Post, 1781.

Dublin University Magazine, vol. xviii (1841) (see under [Wilde, Sir W.]).

European Magazine, 1788.

Faulkner's Dublin Journal, 1749.

Fitzmaurice, Lord Edmond, *The life of Sir William Petty.* 1895.

The writings of Benjamin Franklin, ed. A. H. Smyth, vol. v, New York, 1907.

Furlong, E. J., 'The varying visual sizes of the moon', *Astronomy and Space,* ii (1972), 215-7.

A general dictionary, historical and critical; in which a new and accurate translation of that of . . . Mr Bayle is included, ed. J. P. Bernard and others. 10 vols. 1734-41.

Gentleman's Magazine, 1842.

Gill, Conrad, *The rise of the Irish linen industry.* Oxford, 1925.

Grattan, Henry, *His speeches in the Irish and imperial parliament,* ed. by his son. 4 vols. Dublin, 1822.

Gunther, R. W. T., *Early science in Oxford,* vols. iv, xii, xiii. Oxford, 1912, 1925, 1939.

Gilbert, J. T., *A history of the city of Dublin.* 3 vols. 1854-9.

Harris, Walter, *The history of the writers of Ireland.* Dublin, 1764.

Hogarth, William, *The genuine works of William Hogarth, illustrated . . .,* ed. John Nicholls and George Steevens, vol. i, 1808.

Hoppen, K. T., *The common scientist in the seventeenth century: a study of the Dublin Philosophical Society, 1683-1708.* 1970.

Kaufman, Lloyd, and Roch, Irvin, 'The moon illusion', *Scientific American,* 207 (1962), 120-30.

Kearney, H. F., 'The political background to English mercantilism, 1695-1700', *Economic History Review,* 2nd ser., xi (1959), 484-96.

Kelly, Patrick, 'Locke and Molyneux: the anatomy of a friendship', *Hermathena,* cxxvi (1979), 38-54.

Kelly, Patrick, 'The MS. of the printer's copy of William Molyneux's *Case of Ireland stated*', *Long Room,* xvi (1980), 6-13.

Kelly, Patrick, 'The Irish woollen export prohibition act of 1699: Kearney revisited', *Irish Economic and Social History,* vii (1980), 22-44.

King, C. S., *A great archbishop of Dublin, William King, D.D., 1650-1729.* 1908.

Leibniz, Gottfried, *Nouveaux essais sur l'entendement humain* in *Oeuvres philosophiques de feu M. Leibniz.* Amsterdam and Leipzig, 1765; trans. A. G. Langley. 2 vols. New York, 1896.

Lucas, Charles, *A tenth address to the free citizens and free-holders of the city of Dublin.* Dublin, 1748.

Luce, A. A., *Berkeley and Malebranche.* 1934.

McCracken, J. L., *The Irish parliament in the eighteenth century.* Dundalk, 1971.

McLysaght, Edward, *Irish life in the seventeenth century, after Cromwell.* 2nd edn. Cork, 1950.

Mahaffy, J. P., *The plate in Trinity College, Dublin.* Dublin, 1918.

Manning, P. I., and others, *The geology of Belfast and the Lagan valley.* 2nd edn. Belfast, 1970.

Maxwell, Constantia, *A history of Trinity College, Dublin, 1591-1892.* Dublin, 1946.

Molyneux, Sir Capel, Bt., *An account of the family and descendants of Sir Thomas Molyneux, Kt., Chancellor of the Exchequer in Ireland to Queen Elizabeth.* Privately printed, Evesham, 1820.

Molyneux, Sir Capel, Bt., (ed.), *Anecdotes of the life of the celebrated patriot and philosopher Wm. Molyneux, author of the Case of Ireland: Published from a manuscript written by himself.* Privately printed, Dublin, 1803.

Moody, T. W., Martin, F. X., and Byrne, F. J., (ed.), *A new history of Ireland,* vol. iii: 'Early Modern Ireland'. Oxford, 1976.

Morgan, M. J., *Molyneux's question: vision, touch, and the philosophy of perception.* Cambridge, 1977.

Neuberger, Hans, *Introduction to physical meteorology.* State College, Penn., 1951.

Park, Désirée, 'Locke and Berkeley on the Molyneux problem', *Journal of the History of Ideas,* xxx (1969), 253-60.

Piper, David, (ed.), *Catalogue of seventeenth-century portraits in the National Portrait Gallery.* 1963.

Pope, Alexander, *Minor Poems,* ed. Norman Ault. 1954.

Price, D. J., 'The early instruments of Trinity College, Cambridge', *Annals of Science,* viii (1952), 1-12.

Priestley, Joseph, *The history and present state of discovery relating to vision, light and colours.* 1772.

Reid, Thomas, *An inquiry into the human mind,* Edinburgh, 1764, in *The works of Thomas Reid, D.D.: now fully collected . . .,* ed. Sir William Hamilton, Bt. Edinburgh, 1846.

Robbins, Caroline, *The eighteenth-century commonwealthman.* Cambridge, Mass., 1959.

Saunderson, Nicholas, *The elements of algebra, in ten books.* Cambridge, 1740.

Simms, J. G., 'The bishops' banishment act of 1697', *Irish Historical Studies,* xvii (1970), 185-99.

Simms, J. G., *Colonial Nationalism, 1698-1776.* Cork, 1976.

Simms, J. G., 'Dublin in 1685', *Irish Historical Studies,* xiv (1965), 212-26.

Simms, J. G., *Jacobite Ireland, 1685-91.* 1969.

Simms, J. G., 'John Toland (1670-1722), a Donegal heretic', *Irish Historical Studies,* xvi (1969), 304-20.

Simms, J. G., *The Williamite confiscation in Ireland, 1690-1703.* 1956.

Smith, R. S., *A complete system of optics, in four books.* 2 vols. Cambridge, 1738.

Strickland, W. G., *A dictionary of Irish artists.* 2 vols. 1913.

Swift, Jonathan, *The works of Jonathan Swift,* ed. Herbert Davis, vols. ix-x. Oxford, 1968, 1966.

Taylor, E. G. R., 'The English atlas of Moses Pitt', *Geographical Magazine,* xcv (1940), 292-9.

Taylor, W. B. S., *The history of the University of Dublin.* Dublin, 1845.

Turbayne, Colin, 'Berkeley and Molyneux on retinal images', *Journal of the History of Ideas,* xvi (1955), 345-54.

Voltaire, F. M. A. de, *Eleméns de la philosophie de Newton, mis à la portée de tout le monde,* Amsterdam, 1738; trans. as *The elements of Newton's philosophy,* 1738.

Walton, Clifford, *A history of the British standing army, A.D. 1660 to 1700.* 1894.

[Wilde, Sir William], 'Gallery of illustrious Irishmen, no. XIII: Sir Thomas Molyneux, bart., M.D., F.R.S.', *Dublin University Magazine,* xviii (1841), 305-27, 470-90, 604-19, 744-64. (Prints numerous extracts from correspondence &c.).